SIRTFOOD DIET

COOKBOOK

Beginners Guide To Easy And Healthy Sirtfood
Diet Recipes. Activate Your Skinny Gene And
Burn Fat, Promote Weight Loss And Live
Healthy

Gary Philips

ISBN: 9798636239581

Limit of Liability

The information in this book is solely for informational purposes, not as a medical instruction to replace the advice of your physician or as a replacement for any treatment prescribed by your physician. The author and publisher do not take responsibility for any possible consequences from any treatment, procedure, exercise, dietary modification, action or application of medication which results from reading or following the information contained in this book.

If you are ill or suspect that you have a medical problem, we strongly encourage you to consult your medical, health, or other competent professional before adopting any of the suggestions in this book or drawing inferences from it.

This book and the author's opinions are solely for informational and educational purposes. The author specifically disclaims all responsibility for any liability, loss, or risk, personal or otherwise which is incurred as a consequence, directly or indirectly, of the use and application of any of the contents of this book.

DEDICATION

To All who desire to live And Eat Healthy

TABLE OF CONTENT

INTRODUCTION..1

What is Sirt food? 1

Who Came Up With The Sirtfood Diet? 3

How Do We Take Advantage Of Sirtuins?......................3

What Foods Can Activate Sirtuins?...............................4

What Else Should You Eat? 5

The List Of 20 Top sirtfoods" 6

Is The Sirtfood Diet Good For You?................................9

Sirtfood Diet Is Executed In Two Phases......................10

The Sirtfood Diet Science 11

    Combining Exercise With The Sirtfood Diet..............11

    Exercise During The First Few Weeks 11

Why Eat SirtFoods?...13

Benefits Of Sirtfoof Diet..14

SIRTFOOD DIET RECIPES...17

    Sirtfood Green Juice...18

    Sirtfood Green Tea Smoothie 20

    Melon And Grape Smoothie 20

    Blackcurrant Kale Smoothie.....................................21

    Blackberry Lime Smoothie 22

Green Herbs Sirtfood Smoothie 22

Blackberry Smoothie 23

SIRTFOOD BREAKFAST 24

Apple Blackcurrant Compote Pancakes 25

Blueberry Oats Pancakes 26

Muesli Yoghurt Breakfast 28

Omelette Fold 29

Sirtfood Shakshuka 31

Cherry Tomatoes Red Pesto Porridge 33

Sautéed Veggies Bowl 34

Chocolate Oats Granola 36

Green Chia Spinach Pudding 38

Blackcurrant And Raspberry Breakfast 40

Kale Mushroom Scramble 42

Walnut Medjool Porridge 43

Avocado Tofu Breakfast Salad 44

Buckwheat Coconut Overnight Porridge 46

SirtFood Main 48

Tuscan Carrot Bean Stew 49

Chicken And Turmeric Salad 51

Baked Cod Marinated In Miso With Greens 52

Chicken Breast With Chilli Salsa And Red Onions 55

Mushrooms With Buckwheat Kasha And Olives 56

Asian Prawn Tofu 58

Potatoes And Grilled Beef..60

Butternut, Lamb Tagine 63

Buckwheat Kasha With Onions Mushrooms.............64

Avocado-Adzuki Bean Lettuce Cups..........................65

Buckwheat And Red Onion Kale Dhal 66

Spicy Chickpea With Baked Potatoes Stew..............68

Baked Chicken With Walnut 69

PORK PAK CHOI..71

Sirtfood Pasta Salad 72

Beef Red Onion Potatoes Burgers............................73

Braised Carrots Puy Lentils 74

Sweet Potato Hummus With Bean Falafel And
Couscous..75

Baked Salmon 79

Buckwheat Noodles With Stir-Fry Prawn.................80

Buckwheat Pasta With Prawn And Arrabbiata Sauce
....82

Baked Mackerel Fillets With Potatoes 83

Buckwheat Noodles With Chicken Miso Dressing 85

Strawberry Dates Avocado Buckwheat Tabouleh.....88

Tofu Curry And Kale, Edamame 90

Salmon Salad With Creamy Mayo Dressing 91

Chicken & Kale Curry Sirtfood..................................94

SIRTFOOD SOUP RECIPES...95

Cannellini Bean And Kale Soup 97

Tofu Buckwheat Soba Noodles Carrots And Kale Soup
....98

Carrots Lentil Rosemary Soup...............................100

Sirtfood Vegetable Soup 101

SALAD RECIPES..103

Walnuts Avocado Salad 104

Poached Pear Salad With Dijon Vinegar Dressing...105

Steak Arugula Strawberry Salad.............................107

Super Fruit Salad...108

Sirtfood Salmon Lentils Salad................................110

Blueberry Kale Salad With Ginger Lime Dressing....111

Fancy Chicken Salad...113

Olive, Tomato, Yellow Pepper, Red Onion, Cucumber
Slices And Feta SKEWERS...114

Sesame Soy Chicken Salad 115

Salmon Chicory Rocket Super Salad........................116

Fresh Chopped Salad With Vinegar 117

King Prawns Prawn Parcels 118

SIRTFOOD SNACKS AND BITES 120

Buckwheat Feta Apple Galettes..............................122

Chicken Skewers With Creamy sauce 125

Cocoa Cupcakes With Icing 126

Easy Sirtfood Bites 128

Roasted Salad..129

Tuna And Avocado Kale Stuffed Snacks..................130

Cucumber Tuna Snacks 132

Malabar Sirtfood Prawns 133

INTRODUCTION

What Is Sirtfood?

Sirtfood is the latest trendy diet online after a popular singer like Adele lost 30 pounds just by following the Sirtfood diet. The sirtfood diet was developed by 2 celebrity nutritionists in the U k and since then gained a lot of popularity. Sirtfood diet is a diet rich in sirtuin activators. Sirtuins is a collection of 7 proteins that is responsible for balancing several functions in the body. This group of proteins is found in the body and can also be increased through some natural plant compounds called polyphenols, consuming the kinds of nutrients in these plants can help elevate the amount of these sirtuins proteins in the body. Sirtuins are argued to promote cellular restoration and repair, they can also help balance your metabolism, burn fat and boost muscle.

Who Came Up With The Sirtfood Diet?

Two health consultants and celebrity nutritionists Glen Matten and Aidan Goggins based in the UK wrote about The Sirtfood Diet. This diet concentrates more on a healthy eating pattern rather than just losing weight. This diet is divided into two phase, you are expected to consume three sirtfood green juices and one sirtfood meal in this first phase and one sirtfood green juices with two sirtfood-balanced rich meals in phase two. The idea behind this revolutionary diet plan is that consuming this sirtfood juice and balanced sirtfood meal will help turn on your "skinny gene". According to urban dictionary "skinny gene" is a sequence of DNA which predisposes a person to be thin regardless of said person eating mass quantities of food and not working out.

How Do We Take Advantage Of Sirtuins?

So the big question is how can we activate sirtuins and benefit from it? In general, we cannot but agree that exercise and fasting can help activate sirtuins in the body. But the only set back is that both can be very exhausting, having to maintain well followed through exercise routine or either food restriction. Exercise needs a lot of effort to effectively loss weight, while calories restriction can leave you feeling fatigued or cause muscle loss, irritability hunger and loss of stamina metabolic process; with these few shortcomings, achieving an overall goal might not be as easy as it sounds. As a matter of fact, proteins belonging to the sirtuin family are helpful as anti-ageing agents.

A research was carried out in 2013 between conventional modern diet and Mediterranean-style diet complemented with either nuts or extra-virgin olive oil the reforms that was premised on the findings is called PREDIMED. The Mediterranean diet group showed to have slashed diabetes and heart disease by a massive 30 percent with a significant reduction in risk associated with obesity. Although, it did not come as a surprise, but a further investigation carried out based on the general detail pointed out that both diet had no difference in calorie, carbohydrate or fat intake. Amazing, isn't it?

We are made to understand that there are natural compounds called polyphenols present in some plants that have enormous benefits for our health. Participant that consumed the highest amount of plants with these polyphenols within in the period of five years had 37 percent lesser deaths when compared to participant who ate the least.

Some of these selected polyphenols are capable of switching on our sirtuin genes without needing to exercise of fast.

Although, all Polyphenols are not the same so will not give the same result when you consume. Without any doubt, polyphenols are helpful in staying healthy and slim.

What Foods Can Activate Sirtuins?

With our overall knowledge about plants that contain polyphenols, serving as activation agent for sirtuin. Our whole interest is stimulated towards how to get the highest amount of sirtuin-activating polyphenols incorporated into our diet.

This premise gave birth to the revolutionary Sirtfood Diet, a modern way of eating delicious foods while activating sirtuins. One good thing about Sirtfood Diet is you do not need to cut out carbs, eat low fat or count calories. However, at the first phase, it is stated that combining sirtfoods with calories restriction may activate the body to raise a higher levels of sirtuins. Sirtfood Diet is characterized by eating the foods your love and still reaping the benefits of the diet. Now tell me, if you can eat what you love eating and still lose weight, is it not a diet worth embracing?

What Else Should You Eat?

You can combine the Sirtfoods with protein for a meal. Each meal can be accompanied with oily fish. Just to stress it out; a moderate dairy consumption is perfectly okay"
It is good to understand that the Sirtfood diet does not concentrate on what not to eat; however, there is a need to avoid processed and sugary food or fish that are high in mercury.

The List Of 20 Top sirtfoods"

Coffee
Capers
Blueberries
Citrus fruits
Red chicory
Medjool dates
Lovage
Bird's eye chili
Arugula (rocket)
Apples
Walnuts
Turmeric
Buckwheat
Matcha green tea
Dark chocolate (85% cocoa)
Extra virgin olive oil

Parsley
Soy
Onions
Strawberries
Red wine
Kale

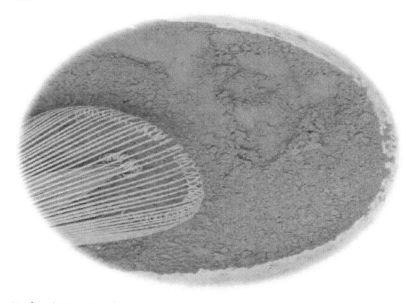

Sirtfood Diet Snacks

Fruits:
Kumquats
Rasberries
Plums
Grape (red)
Goji berries
Cranberries
Apples
Blackcurrant
Blackberries

Vegetables:

Watercress
Shallots
Pak choi (Boy choy)
Onion (white)
Green beans
Endive lettuce
Chicory (yellow)
Broccoli
Asparagus
Artichokes

Other:
Haricot beans
Wholemeal flour
Quinoa
Sunflower seed
Sage
Pistachios
Chives
Peppermint
Ginger
Peanuts
Oregano
Dill
Corn (pop corn)
Chai seeds
Chestnut
Cannellini beans
Broad beans

Some excellent healthy choices of snacks on the sirtfood diet include:
Oat cakes with almond butter
Pecan nuts
Carrots
Cucumber and hummus
Dried figs
Grapefruit
kiwi fruit
Pear
Apple
Edamame
Olives

Is The Sirtfood Diet Good For You?

A strong advantage of the diet is that all the food you can eat on the diet plan has the essential mineral, vitamin and nutrient that you need to stay healthy.
The sirtfood diet can turn on your "skinny gene", super-charge weight loss and prevent diseases.

Sirtfood Diet Is Executed In Two Phases

PHASE ONE:
Phase One lasts for seven days and involves lots of green juice and calorie restriction to 1,000 per day for the first 3 days. You consume 3 sirtfood green juices per day along with one sirtfood balanced meal. During the last 4 (4-7) days of the phase one, you are expected to increase your calories intake to 1,500 consisting of 2 sirtfood green juices and 2 sirtfood balanced meal per day. The idea

is to jump-start your weight loss and achieve a total weight loss of 3.2 kg (7 pounds) in seven days.

PHASE TWO:

After the first phases you are ushered into the second phase which last for 14-day. This stage is more like the maintenance stage; the focus of this stage is not on calories or whatsoever but rather on well-balanced sirt food meals and reasonable portions. The phase features one sirt food green juice and three well-balanced sirt food meals accompanied by 2 sirtfood bite snacks. It is also advised to follow a daily 30 minutes of activity for five days per week. After the second phase, you may decide to repeat the phases from the beginning as you wish for further weight loss. You will find a lot of sirtfood recipes to choose from in this cookbook.

The Sirtfood Diet Science

Sirtfood diet is a diet that can help you activate your 'skinny gene' doorways which are usually activated by exercise and fasting. The best way to embrace a diet plan is to find a healthy one that will not deprive you of eating what you enjoy eating, also flexible enough not to overwork you with excessive exercise. That's what the sirtfood does; by eating the kind of food that contains polyphenols, you activate your sirtuin just as you would when you fast and exercise.

Combining Exercise With The Sirtfood Diet

For so many people, following a healthy eating habit is as difficult as hiking a mountain, they usually give-up within few weeks of being on the diet-this is a more reason to follow a diet pattern that is less restrictive and can become a way of life rather than a one-off fad diet. Although, people differ in lots of ways, some of us might not struggle so much following through with a weight loss diet, others find it too challenging. The Sirtfood diet is an easy way to assist those that find it a bit difficult to follow through a diet plan to achieve weight loss. The question is, is it advisable to combine exercise with Sirtfood diet or completely avoid it?

Exercise During The First Few Weeks

It is advisable to either reduce or stop exercise during the first week or two of the diet because your body might not be able to cope with the initial changes in fewer calories intake. Be sensitive to what your body is telling you, if you feel you do not have enough energy or feeling fatigued, then do not exercise. Stick to the initial science behind the sirt diet of eating food that can activate your sirtuin with daily consumption of vegetables, fruits, fiber and protein. Once the diet becomes a way of life, then you can introduce few workouts.

Mind you, it's best to consume protein after one hour of your workout. Protein can help you recover quickly after exercise, reduces soreness and repairs muscles.

Why Eat SirtFoods?

Let's get one thing straight! Sirtuins was discovered many years ago but the SirtFoods diet came to light in 2003 in a ground breaking study when it was discovered by researchers that resveratrol, a compound found in red wine and red-grapeskin, significantly increase the lifecycle of yeast. Generally, there are lot of researches that needs to be carried out before we can fully understand all the benefits of this diet. So far, through research people are getting to understand the full benefits of these powerful foods; majorly foods already enjoyed, from strawberries to red wine or cocoa. The natural components of these foods have the ability to mimick skinny genes" in our bodies as fasting and exercise does, they can also suppress appetite and build muscle. There is no argument whatsoever about the health benefits of eating fruits and vegetables; they are great source of rich vitamins, minerals and protein.

In contrast, there is a clash of opinion as a few people still believe they cannot get all the required protein to maintain muscle mass from just plants, hereby embracing meats and fish into their meal; without any need to argue that fruits and vegetables are good source of protein. However, following a sirtfood diet does not mean you can only eat foods that are highly sirtuin concentrated or automatic make you a vegetarian. Eating meat, fish, milk, cheese, eggs etc are other good source of getting enough protein in your body. The sirtfood diet does not forbid you from enjoying food you love to eat; in fact no food is left behind. The idea is eating healthy by reducing some harmful foods like high carb or processed foods and replacing them with more of sirtuin foods. One of the disadvantage of carb is the constant cravings; by substituting high carb food with these special kind of protein, you can put an end to carb craving, you will no longer feel hungry as you used to because sirtfood diet naturally suppress your craving. Appetite suppression and calorie deprivation will lead to weight loss, your insulin level will drop, your blood sugar level will reduce, and you will feel healthier and more alive. A good diet should not only focus on weight loss and neglect the overall health. It is pointless to follow a diet that make you lose weight rapidly but jeopardize your overall health. The sirt diet will help you lower blood sugar level and drop insulin level, so you do not need to worry about most heath problems like inflammation, diabetes, cancer etc, which are all caused by poor nutrition.

Now, you have a reason to embrace the sirtfood diet; set a long term goal and make sirt food a lifestyle.
Don't know what to eat? You will find plenty sirtfood recipes in this book to help you get started and stay on course.

Benefits Of Sirtfoof Diet

Sirtfood Diet Helps To Maintain Muscle Mass:
When people try to lose weight, chances are they lose muscle also. We all need the right amount of protein to preserve our muscle mass. The sirtfood diet is a combination of healthy protein called sirtuins, these proteins help you to maintain your muscle mass while losing weight, so it does not make you lack energy or leave you feeling too weak.

Sirtfood Diet Protects The Body From Chronic Disease:

You can quite agree with me that about 70 percent of deaths we have these days are associated with chronic disease; these chronic diseases are largely cause by the kind of food we eat. People have formed the habit of not eating healthy; with vast number of processed foods a lot of people consume on a daily basis, these foods accumulate fats and toxic, causing our blood and insulin level to rise. One of the reasons for bad health is lack of sirtuin in our body. Our body can heal itself if we activate the level of sirtuin in our body. Sirtuin can help protect the muscle cells around the heart which leads to improved heart function.

Sirtfood Diet helps to reverse ageing and promotes glowing skins: According to science, autophagy function to repair and replace damaged cells part in the body, part of this repair is done through AMPK activators (small molecules that mimic cellular) these kinds of protein coordinates metabolic pathways which help maintain adequate nutrient provision with energy demand. To make it simple, if all the damaged cells in your body can be repaired and start functioning optimally, then you can reverse aging. The autophagy can help slow down the effect of aging greatly and the good news is autophagy can be activated through sirtuin.

Sirtfood Diet helps super-charge rapid weight loss and turn on your skinny gene:
One of the benefits of sirtfood diet is the ability to help maintain weight loss over a sustainable period of time. Most people following other diet end up going back to their old eating habits and eventually recover all the weight they lose initially. The sirtfood diet will not just help you lose weight in a short time; it helps you lose weight in a sustainable way. The secret behind every good diet is to help lose weight and feel healthy at the same time. Eating foods

high in sirtuin activators switch on your skinny gene and activate your fat-burning powers for sustained weight loss.

SIRTFOOD DIET RECIPES

Sirtfood Green Juice

Ready time: 4 minutes

Servings: 1

INGREDIENTS

Half level teaspoon of matcha green tea

Half lemon juice

Half medium green apple

2–3 (150g) large green celery stalks, with the leaves

Very small handful (5g) lovage leaves (optional)

Very small (5g) handful of flat-leaf parsley

Large (30g) handful of rocket

2 (75g) large handfuls of kale

INSTRUCTIONS

1. Mix together the parsley, kale, lovage (optional) and rocket. Turn the juicer and add everything into it, then juice until has been juiced. It should give you about 50ml of juice.

2. Add apple and celery and juice, if desired, peel the lemon and juice along with the apple and celery. (I prefer to squeeze the lemon by hand and add into the juicer along with other ingredients). This should give you a total of 250ml of juice.

3. Add a little amount of juice along with the matcha into a glass, mix thoroughly until dissolved. Add the remaining juice and stir once again to mix well. You can add a little water if desired. Enjoy!

Note: Matcha contains moderate amounts of caffeine so we advice to only use for the first and second juice of the day.

Nutrition Information:

kcal: 230

Net carbs: 30 g

Fat: 12g

Fiber: 10 g

Protein: 8g

Sirtfood Green Tea Smoothie

Ready Time: 3 minutes

Servings: 2

INGREDIENTS

2 tsp of honey

6 ice cubes

1/2 tsp of vanilla bean paste

2 tsp of matcha green tea powder

250 ml of milk

2 ripe bananas

INSTRUCTIONS

1. Combine together the entire ingredients in a blender until you have a smooth mixture. Serve in two glasses.

Note: If you do not have vanilla bean paste, simply use a small scrape of the seeds from a vanilla pod. Matcha powder can be found in specialist Asian or tea shops.

Melon And Grape Smoothie

Ready Time: 2 minutes

Servings: 1

INGREDIENTS

100 grams of cantaloupe melon, peeled, seed removed and cut into chunks

100 grams red seedless grapes

30 grams of young spinach leaves, stalks removed

½ peeled cucumber, seeded and roughly chopped

INSTRUCTIONS

1. Combine together the entire ingredients in a blender until you have a smooth mixture. Serve in glass.

Nutrition Information:
kcal: 125
Net carbs: 29 g
Fat: 3.44g
Fiber: 4.4 g
Protein: 0.74g

Blackcurrant Kale Smoothie

Ready time: 3 minutes

Servings: 2

INGREDIENTS

6 ice cubes

40 grams of blackcurrants, washed and remove stalks

1 ripe banana

10 baby kale leaves, stalks removed

1 cup of freshly made matcha green tea

2 tsp of honey

INSTRUCTIONS

1. Dissolve the honey in fresh and warm green tea. Blend together the entire ingredients in a food processor until mixture is smooth. Serve right away.

Nutrition Information:
kcal: 86
Net carbs: 14 g
Fat: 2.9g
Fiber: 11 g
Protein: 9g

Blackberry Lime Smoothie

Serving: 2

INGREDIENTS:

½ teaspoon of vanilla

2 tablespoon of coconut oil

1 fresh lime juiced

1 large of bunch of kale

½ cup of frozen strawberries

1 cup of frozen blackberries

1 ½ cups of almond or coconut milk, unsweetened

1 tablespoon of raw almond butter (Optional)

INSTRUCTIONS

1. Start by blending the coconut milk and kale, then pour in other ingredients, and blend until you have a smooth mixture.

Green Herbs Sirtfood Smoothie

Prep time: 5 minutes

Servings: 1

INGREDIENTS:

1/2 teaspoon of Chia seeds, ground (optional)

1 whole fresh Lime juice

1 cup of water

1 1/2 tsp minced ginger root (optional)

1/4 cup of diced Pineapple, banana or mango

1 medium Pear

2 medium celery stalk

1/2 cup of cucumber

1/2 cup of cilantro (coriander)

1/2 cup of kale

INSTRUCTIONS

1. Combine all the ingredients in a blender and blend until you have smooth mixture.

Nutrition Information without the pear:

kcal: 69, Net carbs: 14 g

Fat: 0.37g, Fiber: 2.2 g, Protein: 1.9g

SIRTFOOD BREAKFAST

Apple Blackcurrant Compote Pancakes

Prep time: 5 minutes
Cook time: 15 minutes
Servings: 4

INGREDIENTS

For the compote:

3 tbsp of water
2 tbsp of caster sugar
120 grams of blackcurrants, washed and stalks removed

For The Apple Pancakes:

2 tsp of light olive oil
2 egg whites
300 ml of semi-skimmed milk
2 apples, peeled, cored and cut into small pieces
Pinch of salt
2 tbsp of caster sugar
1 tsp of baking powder
125 grams plain flour
75 grams of porridge oats

INSTRUCTIONS

1. In a small pan, add the blackcurrants, water and sugar. Bring to a gentle boil and let it cook for 10 to 15 minutes.
2. In a large bowl, place the flour, oats, baking powder, salt and caster sugar, mix well.
3. Add in the apple, stir and gently fold in semi-skimmed milk until mixture is smooth.
4. Beat the egg whites until stiff peaks forms and then gently whisk into the flour mixture. Pour batter into a jug.
5. Heat half teaspoon of oil over medium-high heat in a non-stick frying pan. Add about 1/4 of the batter into the pan. Cook pancake until golden brown on both sides. Repeat with the remaining batter. Drizzle the blackcurrant compote over pancakes and serve.

Nutrition Information:

kcal: 337
Net carbs: 40 g
Fat: 9.82g
Fiber: 6.2 g, Protein: 32g

Blueberry Oats Pancakes

Prep time: 5 minutes

Cook time: 5 minutes

Servings: 4

INGREDIENTS

225 grams of blueberries

¼ tsp of salt

2 tsp of baking powder

150 grams of rolled oats

6 eggs

6 bananas

INSTRUCTIONS

1. Pulse the rolled oats for 1 minute in a (dry) high-speed blender to form oat flour.

2. Add in the eggs, bananas, salt and baking powder and process for 2 minutes until it forms a smooth batter.

3. Pour the batter into a large bowl and gently stir in the blueberries. Let sit for at least 10 minutes to activate the baking powder.

4. Add a large spoonful of butter to the frying pan over a medium high heat. Scoop a few tablespoons of the batter and cook until nicely golden underneath. Flip pancake and cook the other side.

Nutrition Information:

kcal: 494

Net carbs: 68 g

Fat: 11.3g

Fiber: 6.2 g

Protein: 22.23g

Muesli Yoghurt Breakfast

Ready time: 3 minutes

Servings: 1

INGREDIENTS

100g plain Greek, coconut or soya yoghurt

100g of hulled and chopped strawberries

10g of cocoa nibs

15g chopped walnuts

40g of pitted and chopped Medjool dates

15g of coconut flakes or desiccated coconut

10g of buckwheat puffs

20g of buckwheat flakes

INSTRUCTIONS

1. Mix together the cocoa nibs, buckwheat flakes, coconut flakes, buckwheat puffs, Medjool dates and walnuts. Add the yoghurt and strawberries when ready to serve.

Nutrition Information:

kcal: 368

Net carbs: 49 g

Fat: 11.5g

Fiber: 7.4 g

Protein: 16.54g

Omelette Fold

Prep time: 3 minutes

Cook time: 5 minutes

Servings: 1

INGREDIENTS

1 tsp of extra virgin olive oil

5 grams of thinly sliced parsley

35 grams of thinly sliced red chicory

3 medium eggs

50 grams of streaky bacon, cut into thin strips

INSTRUCTIONS

1. Cook the bacon strips in hot non-stick frying pan over high heat until crispy. Remove and drain any excess fat on a kitchen paper. Prepare the pan for another use.

2. Beat the eggs in a small bowl and mix with the parsley and chicory. Mix the drained bacon through the egg mixture.

3. Heat the olive oil in a non-stick pan; add the bacon/egg mixture. Cook until omelette is set. Loose the omelette around the edges with a spatula and fold into half moon and serve.

Nutrition Information:
kcal: 471
Net carbs: 3.3 g
Fat: 38.72g
Fiber: 1.5 g
Protein: 27g

Sirtfood Shakshuka

Prep time: 40 minutes
Total time: 40 minutes
Servings: 1

INGREDIENTS

2 Medium eggs
1 tbsp of chopped parsley
30 grams of Kale, stems removed and chopped roughly
400 grams of tinned chopped tomatoes
1 tsp of Paprika
1 tsp of ground turmeric
1 tsp of ground cumin
1 finely chopped Bird's eye chilli
30 grams of finely chopped celery
1 finely chopped garlic clove
40 grams of Red onion, finely chopped
1 tsp of extra virgin olive oil

INSTRUCTIONS

1. Heat the olive oil over a medium–low heat in a small, deep frying pan, add the garlic, onion, chili, celery, and spices and fry for 1–2 minutes.

2. Add chopped tomatoes into the pan, simmer gently, stirring occasionally for about 20 minutes.

3. Place the kale and keep cooking for another 5 minutes. Add a little water if the sauce is too thick. Stir in the parsley.

4. Make 2 small holes into the sauce and add the eggs into each hole. Turn heat down to its lowest, place a lid on pan. Cook for about 10 to 12 minutes until whites and yolk are firm. (Although, depending on how you like your eggs) Serve immediately.

Nutrition Information:

kcal: 269

Net carbs: 16 g

Fat: 12.32g

Fiber: 7.4 g

Protein: 18.81g

Cherry Tomatoes Red Pesto Porridge

Prep Time: 10 minutes

Cook Time: 5 minutes

Servings: 2

INGREDIENTS:

Salt, pepper

1 tablespoon of hemp seed

1 tablespoon of pumpkin seed

2 tablespoon of nutritional yeast

1 tablespoon of sun-dried tomato-walnut pesto

1 teaspoon of tahini

1 scallion

1 cup of sliced cherry tomatoes

1 cup of chopped kale

1 teaspoon of dried basil

1, 5 teaspoon of dried oregano

1, 5-2 cups of veggie stock (or water)

½ cup of couscous

½ cup of oats

INSTRUCTIONS

1. In a small cooking pot, add oats, oregano, vegetable stock, basil, couscous, pepper and salt and cook for about 5 minutes on medium heat stirring frequently until porridge is creamy and soft.

2. Add chopped kale but reserve a bit for garnish, tomatoes and sliced scallion. Cook for additional 1 minute, stir in pesto, tahini, and nutritional yeast.

Top with the reserved kale, pumpkin and hemp seeds plus cherry tomatoes, Enjoy!

Nutrition Information:

kcal: 259, Net carbs: 36 g, Fat: 7.68g

Fiber: 7.4 g, Protein: 14.26g

Sautéed Veggies Bowl

Prep time: 5 minutes

Cook time: 5 minutes

Serving: 1

INGREDIENTS:

For tofu scramble:

1 tablespoon of water

Dash of soy sauce

Pepper and salt

1 teaspoon of turmeric

1 serving medium of crumbled firm tofu

For the Sautéed Veggies:

1/2 cup of red onions, diced

1 cup of mushrooms, sliced

1 big handful of kale, de-stemmed and chopped

For the Bowls

1/2 cup of cooked brown rice

1/2 avocado, pitted

Salsa

INSTRUCTIONS

1. Mix together the tofu scramble ingredients in a small dish, set aside.

2. Add a splash of water in a skillet over medium-high heat; add the onions, mushrooms and kale. Cook, stirring periodically, for about 5-8 minutes or until it is evenly brown and soft. Set aside in a bowl.

3. Using the same skillet, pour in the tofu mixture and cook until it starts to brown and heated through for 5 minutes.

4. Transfer tofu scramble into a bowl, add the mushrooms/kale mixture, top with avocado, brown rice and salsa. Serve with flatbreads, buckwheat, basmati rice or couscous.

Chocolate Oats Granola

Prep time: 10 minutes

Cook time: 20 minutes

Servings: 8

INGREDIENTS

60 grams of good-quality dark chocolate chips (70%)

2 tbsp of rice malt syrup or maple syrup

1 tbsp of dark brown sugar

20 grams roughly chopped butter

3 tbsp of light olive oil

50 grams of roughly chopped pecans

200 grams of jumbo oats

INSTRUCTIONS

1. Heat-up your oven to 160°C).

2. In a large bowl, mix together pacan and oats. Gently heat the butter, olive oil, rice malt syrup and brown sugar in a small non-stick pan until the sugar and syrup is dissolved and butter melted. Do not allow the mixture boil before removing. Spread the mixture on top the oats and stir very well to coat with the oats.

3. Distribute the oats mixture onto a large parchment lined baking tray, spread out into every corners. You do not need to spread evenly, leave lumps of mixture with spacing.

4. Place tray in the oven and bake until edges are just tinged golden brown, about 20 minutes. Withdraw from the oven and let completely cool on the tray.

5. Once cool, use your finger to break up any lager lumps. Add in the chocolate chips and mix. Serve Chocolate granula with cup of green tea.

Keep leftover in an airtight container, can keep for 2 weeks.

Nutrition Information:

kcal: 244, Net carbs: 20.91 g

Fat: 15.41g, Fiber: 4.6 g, Protein: 5.24g

Green Chia Spinach Pudding

Prep Time: 30 minutes

Chilling Time: 1 minute

Servings: 1

INGREDIENTS:

3 tablespoons of chia seeds

1 Medjool date, slice in half and remove pit

1 handful of fresh spinach

1 cup non-dairy milk (almond, organic soy or coconut)

Toppings

Banana, berries, mango etc

INSTRUCTIONS

1. Blend the spinach, date and milk in a high speed blender until very smooth.

2. Pour the mixture in a bowl over the chia seeds. Stir mixture well, and stirring every now and then for about 15 minutes.

3. Transfer to the fridge and allow to chill at least one hour or overnight.

4. Stir once more, just before serving; top with kiwi, banana, berries, mango, etc.

Enjoy!

Blackcurrant And Raspberry Breakfast

Prep time: 5 minutes

Ready time: 15 minutes

Servings: 2

INGREDIENTS

300 ml of water

2 tbsp of granulated sugar

100 grams of blackcurrants, washed and stalks removed

2 leaves gelatine

100 grams of raspberries, washed

INSTRUCTIONS

1. In two serving glasses or dishes, add the raspberries and set aside.

2. Add cold water in a bowl and place the gelatine leaves to soften.

3. In a small pan, add the blackcurrants with 100 ml of water along with the sugar. Bring to the boil. Let it simmer for five minutes and then turn heat off. Remove and let cool for 2 minutes.

4. Remove the gelatine leaves and squeeze out excess water. Place leaves in the saucepan. Stir constantly until completely dissolved, then add in the remaining water and stir together.

5. Pour liquid over raspberries in the glasses or dishes. Place in the refrigerator for about 3-4 hours or overnight and allow to set.

Note: Best to make the jelly in advance while you wake in the morning to a beautiful meal.

Nutrition Information:
kcal: 76
Net carbs: 13.57 g
Fat: 0.5g
Fiber: 3.3 g
Protein: 4g

Kale Mushroom Scramble

Prep time: 10 minutes
Cook time: 6 minutes
Servings: 1

INGREDIENTS

Optional* Add a seed mixture as a topper and some Rooster Sauce for flavor
5 grams of finely chopped parsley
Handful of thinly sliced button mushrooms
½ thinly sliced bird's eye chilli
1 tsp extra virgin olive oil
20 grams of kale, roughly chopped
1 tsp of mild curry powder
1 tsp of ground turmeric
2 eggs

INSTRUCTIONS

1. Mix together the curry powder, turmeric and a small splash of water to form a light paste.

2. Add the kale to a steamer basket and steam in boiling water for 2– 3 minutes.

3. Heat the oil over medium heat in a frying pan and fry mushrooms and chilli for 2 to 3 minutes until soften and starting to brown.

Walnut Medjool Porridge

Prep time: 10 minutes

Servings: 1

INGREDIENTS

50 grams of strawberries, hulled

1 tsp of walnut butter or 4 chopped walnut halves

35 grams of Buckwheat flakes

1 chopped Medjool date

200 ml of almond or coconut milk, unsweetened

INSTRUCTIONS

1. Add the date and milk into a frying pan over medium low heat, then add in the flakes and cook to your desired consistency.

2. Add in the walnut butter, stir well. Top porridge with strawberries.

Nutrition Information:

kcal: 550

Net carbs: 25 g

Fat: 45g

Fiber: 9 g

Protein: 6.57g

Avocado Tofu Breakfast Salad

Ready time: 5 minutes

Servings: 1

INGREDIENTS

Half a lemon juice

Half a red onion, chopped

2 tomatoes, chopped

One spoon of chili sauce

4 handfuls of baby spinach

A handful of chopped almonds

1 pink chopped grapefruit

1 Avocado, chopped

Half a pack of firm tofu, chopped

2 Tortillas

INSTRUCTIONS

1. Heat the tortillas in the oven for 8 to 10 minutes.

2. Combine tomatoes, tofu and onions with some chilli sauce in a bowl, place inside the refrigerator to cool.

3. Add the avocado, grapefruit and almonds. Mix everything together and place into the bowl.
4. Top with a Squeeze of fresh lemon juice!

Buckwheat Coconut Overnight Porridge

Prep time: 10 minutes
Cook time: 8 minutes
Serving: 4-6
INGREDIENTS:
1/4 tsp of cinnamon
2 tsp of vanilla extract
1 cup of water
3 cups of unsweetened coconut milk or almond or soy
1/4 cup of chia seeds
1 cup of buckwheat groats (not kasha)
Pinch of salt
For the Toppings:
(Optional) 1/2 cup of unsweetened shredded coconut
1 1/2 cup of berries
1/2 cup of walnuts
INSTRUCTIONS
1. In a bowl, combine together the buckwheat groats, coconut milk, chia seeds, cinnamon, water, vanilla extract and salt. Cover bowl with stretch film, transfer to the fridge and let sit overnight.
2. Bring it out in the morning and place it in a pot; cook mixture in the pot for 10-12 minutes, stirring occasionally until your desired thickness is reached. Add the toppings and Serve.

Nutrition Information:
kcal: 400, Net carbs: 47 g, Fat: 17.55g
Fiber: 3.7 g, Protein: 11.19g

SIRTFOOD MAIN

Tuscan Carrot Bean Stew

Prep time: 10 minutes

Cook time: 40 minutes

Servings: 1

INGREDIENTS

40 grams of buckwheat

1 tbsp of roughly chopped parsley

50 grams of kale, roughly chopped

200 grams of tinned mixed beans

1 tsp of tomato purée

400 grams of tin chopped Italian tomatoes

200 ml of vegetable stock

1 tsp of herbes de Provence

(Optional) half bird's eye chilli, finely chopped

1 finely chopped garlic clove

30 grams of celery, trimmed and finely chopped

30 grams of peeled and chopped carrot

50 grams of finely chopped red onion

1 tbsp of extra virgin olive oil

INSTRUCTIONS

1. Gently fry the onion, celery, carrot, chilli (if using), garlic and herbs in hot oil over a low–medium heat in a medium saucepan until the onion is soft.

2. Add the tomato purée, vegetable stock and tomatoes and bring to a boil. Pour in beans and simmer about 30 minutes.

3. Add chopped kale and cook for additional 6 to 10 minutes, until kale is soft, add in chopped parsley.

4. Cook the buckwheat the way instructed in packet directions, drain. Serve cooked buckwheat noodles with bean stew.

Nutrition Information:

kcal: 306, Net carbs: 29 g

Fat: 12.23g, Fiber: 15 g, Protein:9.91g

Chicken And Turmeric Salad

Prep time: 12 minutes

Cook time: 15 minutes

Servings: 1

INGREDIENTS

1 handful of coriander chopped leaves

1 handful of parsley chopped

1/2 sliced avocado

2 tbsp of pumpkin seeds

3 large kale leaves (cut off stems)

2 cups of broccoli florets

Juice of 1/2 lime

1 tsp of lime zest

9-oz of diced up chicken breast

1/2 diced onion

1 tsp of turmeric powder

1 tbsp of coconut oil

1 large minced garlic clove

For the Dressing

½ tsp of sea salt and pepper

½ tsp of wholegrain or Dijon mustard

1 tsp of raw honey

3 tbsp of extra-virgin olive oil

1 small grated garlic clove, or finely diced

3 tbsp of lime juice

INSTRUCTIONS

1. Heat the coconut oil over medium heat in a frying pan. Sauté onion in hot oil for 4 minutes until soft and fragrance. Add in garlic and chicken pieces to the frying pan, cook stirring for about 2 to 3 minutes and breaking apart. Add lime zest, and juice, salt, turmeric and pepper; allow to cook for extra 3 to 4 minutes. Transfer to bowl and set aside.

2. Cook the broccoli florets in boiling water in a small saucepan for 2-3 minutes, rinse with cold water.

3. Pour the pumpkin seeds into the same frying pan earlier used in cooking the chicken. Toast for a few minutes over medium heat, stirring continuously so it does not burn.

4. Combine the dressing ingredients together in a bowl. Place kale into a large salad bowl and spread the dressing over kale in the bowl, tossing until coated. Add in chicken, broccoli florets, herbs, pumpkin seeds, avocado slices, parsley and coriander and toss to coat well.

Baked Cod Marinated In Miso With Greens

Prep time: 50 minutes

Cook time: 25 minutes

Servings: 1

INGREDIENTS

1 tsp of ground turmeric

1/4 cup of buckwheat (40g)

1 tbsp of soy sauce

2 tbsp of roughly chopped parsley, (5g)

1 tsp of sesame seeds

3/4 cup of roughly chopped kale, (50g)

3/8 cup of green beans (60g)

1 tsp of finely chopped fresh ginger

1 finely chopped Thai chili

2 finely chopped garlic cloves

3/8 cup of sliced celery, (40g)

1/8 cup of sliced red onion, (20g)

1 x 7-oz of skinless cod fillet (200g)

1 tbsp of extra virgin olive oil

1 tbsp of mirin

(20g) 3 1/2 tsp of miso

INSTRUCTIONS

1. Mix together 1 tsp of olive oil, miso and mirin. Rub the cod all over with the mixture and let it marinate for half hour.

2. Preheat the oven to 425 degrees F. Once you are done marinating, place the cod in the oven and bake for 10 minutes.

3. While the cod is cooking, pour the remaining olive oil in a large frying pan and heat over medium heat. Stir-fry the onion in the hot oil for a few minutes, add the ginger, celery, kale, garlic, green beans, and chili. Cook stirring frequently and tossing until the kale is cooked through and tender. Add a few drops of water to pan if needed.

4. Cook the buckwheat along with turmeric the way instructed in package instruction.

5. Add the soy sauce, parsley and sesame seeds to the stir-fry. Serve fish with the stir-fry and buckwheat.

Nutrition Information:
kcal: 500
Net carbs: 65 g
Fat: 17.26g
Fiber: 22 g
Protein:24g

Chicken Breast With Chilli Salsa And Red Onions

Prep time: 10 minutes
Cook time: 20 minutes
Servings: 1
INGREDIENTS
50 grams of buckwheat
1 tsp of chopped fresh ginger
20 grams of sliced red onion
50 grams of chopped kale
1 tbsp of extra virgin olive oil
¼ lemon juice
2 tsp of ground turmeric
120 grams of boneless, skinless chicken breast
For the salsa
¼ lemon Juice
5 grams finely chopped parsley
1 tbsp of capers, finely chopped
1 finely chopped bird's eye chilli
130 grams of tomato

INSTRUCTIONS

How To Make The Salsa:

1. Finely chop the tomato, trying to keep as much of the juice as you can.
2. Mix the chopped tomato with the parsley, lemon juice, capers, and chilli.
3. Preheat the oven to 425 F. In a bowl, mix together a little olive oil, 1 tsp. turmeric and lemon juice. Place the chicken breast and marinate for 5–10 minutes.
4. Meanwhile, heat an oven-resistance frying pan over medium high heat until hot, place the chicken and cook until pale golden, about 1 to 1 1/2 minutes on each side.
5. Place the frying pan in the oven and cook until cooked through, for 8–10 minutes. Place pan on a baking tray if you did not use a heat-proof pan. Once cooked, remove chicken from the oven, cover with foil and let sit for five minutes before carving.
6. While the chicken is cooking, add the kale to a steamer and cook for 5 minutes.
7. Add a little oil to a frying pan and cook the ginger and red onions, until soft but not colored. Add in the cooked kale to the frying pan and cook for additional 1 minute.
8. Cook the buckwheat along with the remaining turmeric the way instructed in package instruction. (Takes about 5-8 minutes) Serve chicken alongside the buckwheat, vegetables and salsa.

Nutrition Information:

kcal: 392
Net carbs: 40 g
Fat: 14.26g
Fiber: 7 g
Protein:17.79g

Mushrooms With Buckwheat Kasha And Olives

Prep time: 5 minutes

Cook time: 20 minutes

Servings: 4

INGREDIENTS

1/4 cup of chopped parsley

1/2 cup of black olives sliced

8 ounces of baby bella mushrooms

1 tbsp of olive oil

1 tbsp of almond butter

1 cup of buckwheat groats toasted

2 teaspoon salt

2 tbsp of soy sauce

INSTRUCTIONS

1. Add 2 cups of water, buckwheat, butter and salt in a pot. Bring mixture to a boil, turn heat down and simmer for 20 minutes with the lid on.

2. Add the olive oil to pan over medium high heat. Add in the mushrooms and fry about 10-15 minutes or until lightly browned.

3. Combine together the mushrooms/buckwheat mix, olives, soy sauce and parsley Mix In a large bowl.

Nutrition Information:

kcal: 235

Net carbs: 34 g

Fat: 10.26g

Fiber: 8g

Protein:7.7g

Asian Prawn Tofu

Prep time: 10 minutes
Cook time: 15 minutes
Servings: 5

INGREDIENTS

1 tbsp of good-quality miso paste
20 grams of sushi ginger, chopped
50 grams of cooked water chestnuts, drained
50 grams of rice noodles
100 grams of chopped firm tofu
100 grams of raw tiger prawns
50 grams of bean sprouts
50 grams of broccoli, cut into small florets
1/2 carrot, cut into matchsticks
500 ml of fresh chicken stock, or made with 1 cube
Juice of 1/2 lime
Small handful of coriander, stalks finely chopped (10g)
Small handful of parsley, stalks finely chopped (10g)
1 crushed star anise, or 1/4 tsp of ground anise
1 tsp of tomato purée

INSTRUCTIONS

1. In a large pan, add the chicken stock, star anise, tomato purée, parsley stalks, lime juice and coriander stalks and bring mixture to a simmer, about 10 minutes.
2. Cook the rice noodles according to packet instructions, drain.
3. Add cooked noodles, broccoli, tofu, carrot, prawns, and water chestnuts and gently simmer until the vegetables and prawns are cooked. Turn heat off and stir in the miso paste and sushi ginger. Serve with a sprinkle of coriander and parsley.

Nutrition Information:
kcal: 139, Net carbs: 13 g
Fat: 3.9g, Fiber: 2.8 g, Protein: 11g

Potatoes And Grilled Beef

Prep time: 20 minutes

Cook time: 70 minutes

Servings: 1

INGREDIENTS

100 grams of potatoes, peeled and diced into 2cm cubes

1 tbsp of extra virgin olive oil

5 grams of parsley, finely chopped

50 grams of red onion, sliced into rings

50 grams of kale, chopped

1 clove garlic, finely chopped

120-150 grams of beef fillet, 3.5cm-thick

Steak or 2 cm-thick sirloin steak

40 ml red wine

150 ml beef stock

1 tsp of tomato purée

1 tsp of cornflour, dissolved in 1 tbsp of water

INSTRUCTIONS

1. Preheat the oven to 220ºC.

2. Bring water to a boil in a saucepan and cook the potatoes for about 4-5 minutes, then drain.

3. Add 1 teaspoon of olive oil in the roasting tin and cook the potatoes in the oven about 35 to 45 minutes, turning every 10 minutes. Withdraw the potatoes from the oven, sprinkle well with chopped parsley and mix well.

4. Fry the onion in 1 teaspoon of olive in a frying pan over medium heat until tender and caramelized. Keep warm.

5. Steam the kale for 2-3 minutes in boiling water in a medium saucepan until slightly wilted, then drain. Gently sauté the garlic in half teaspoon of olive oil until soft, about 1 minute. Add in kale and cook until soft, 1-2 minutes. Keep warm.

6. Heat an oven-safe pan over medium heat until hot. Coat the meat in half teaspoon of olive oil and fry to your desired likeness. Set aside to rest.

7. Pour red wine into the hot frying pan and deglaze any brown bit from the pan. Cook until liquid is reduced by half and syrupy with a concentrated flavor.

8. Add tomato purée and beef stock into the pan, bring mixture to the boil.

9. Slowly add the corn flour paste into the pan to thicken the sauce until you have your desired consistency. Stir in any juice from the rested steak and serve with potatoes, kale, onion rings and red wine sauce

Nutrition Information:
kcal:
Net carbs:
Fat:
Fiber:
Protein:

Butternut, Lamb Tagine

Prep time: 15 minutes
Cook time: 1 hour 15 minutes
Servings: 4

INGREDIENTS

2 tbsp of fresh chopped coriander, plus more for garnish
400 grams of tin chickpeas, drained
500 grams of butternut squash, chopped into 1 cm cubes
400 grams of chopped tomatoes tin, plus 1/2 of the liquid from can
100 grams of medjool dates, pitted and chopped
½ tsp of salt
800 grams of lamb neck fillet, cut into 2cm pieces
2 tsp of ground turmeric
1 cinnamon stick
2 tsp of cumin seeds
1 tsp of chilli flakes
3 grated garlic cloves, or crushed
2 cm ginger, grated
1 sliced red onion
2 tbsp of olive oil

INSTRUCTIONS

1. Heat-up the oven to 285 F.

2. In a cast iron skillet or a large oven-safe saucepan with lid, heat about 2 tbsp. of olive oil. Gently cook the onion in hot oil for about 5 minutes, with the lid on until onions are tender but not brown.

3. Add the ginger and grated garlic, cumin, turmeric, cinnamon and chilli. Stir together and cook without the lid for 1 extra minute. You can add a little bit of water to help with the cooking if you fell it's too dry.

4. Add in the lamb pieces; stirring thoroughly so the meat coat in the spices. Add the chopped dates, salt, and tomatoes with half of the liquid from can (100-200ml).

5. Bring to a boil, place the lid then transfer to the preheated oven and cook for 75 minutes.

6. Remove from oven 30 minutes before the final cooking time and add in the drained chickpeas and chopped squash. Stir until everything is well mixed, cover and place back in the oven; cook for the last 30 minutes.

7. Once it's cooked, withdraw and stir in the coriander; best served with flatbreads, buckwheat, basmati rice or couscous.

Nutrition Information:

kcal: 450

Fat: 26g

Fiber: 2.8 g

Protein: 30g

Buckwheat Kasha With Onions Mushrooms

Prep time: 10 minutes

Cook time: 30 minutes

Servings: 4

INGREDIENTS

A small bunch of dill, chopped

Salt and freshly ground black pepper

250 grams of brown mushrooms

1 tbsp of olive oil

A small bunch of parsley, less than dill, chopped

2 tbsp of butter, divided

3 small red onions, thinly sliced

450 ml of chicken stock or vegetable broth (a bit less than 2 cups)

1 egg

150 grams of roasted buckwheat groats

INSTRUCTIONS

1. Lightly whisk the egg in a bowl. Mix in the buckwheat until well mixed.

2. Heat a non stick pan over medium heat, add buckwheat and cook until all the corns are separated and dry, about 3-4 minutes.

3. Transfer the buckwheat to a small saucepan. Add in the stock or broth and bring to a boil, reduce heat and let it simmer for 15 minutes or there about until stock has been absorbed and the buckwheat is soft.

4. Heat the olive oil with 1 tbsp. butter in the pan on low heat; add onions and cook, stirring often for 15 minutes or until tender and golden brown. You can add a few splash of water in between so the onion won't catch.

5. Add in the mushrooms and cook for additional 5-7 minutes or until withered and cooked; season with salt and pepper.

6. Add in buckwheat and stir to coat well. Stir in the remaining butter. Add in chopped parsley and dill. Serve with some green salad.

Nutrition Information:
kcal: 223
Net carbs: 19 g
Fat: 12g
Fiber: 3 g
Protein: 8g

Avocado-Adzuki Bean Lettuce Cups

Ready time: 5 minutes
Serving: 4
INGREDIENTS:
Sea salt (Himalayan, Celtic Grey, or Redmond Real Salt)
1 lime juice
1 avocado
8 butter lettuce leaves or romaine, these make lovely cups
Small handful of chopped cilantro
¼ cup of red onion, minced
1 15-oz can of Adzuki beans, drained and rinsed
Red pepper flakes (optional)
INSTRUCTIONS
1. In a bowl, mash together the red onion and beans. Add chopped cilantro, stir to combine.
2. Spoon the mash beans into lettuce cups and add diced avocado to the top with lime juice; season with red pepper flakes and salt.

Nutrition Information:
kcal: 118
Net carbs: 6 g
Fat: 8g
Fiber: 6 g
Protein: 2.69g

Buckwheat And Red Onion Kale Dhal

Prep time: 5 minutes
Cook time: 25 minutes
Serves: 4

INGREDIENTS

160 grams of buckwheat (or brown rice)
100 grams of kale
200 ml of water
400 ml of coconut milk
160 grams of red lentils
2 tsp of garam masala
2 tsp of turmeric
1 birds eye chilli, seed removed and chopped finely or more to
increase hotness
2 cm grated ginger
3 grated or crushed garlic cloves
1 small sliced red onion
1 tbsp of olive oil

INSTRUCTIONS

1. Heat a deep large saucepan over low heat; add olive oil and sauté
the onion in hot oil for 5 minutes with the lid until softened.

2. Add the garlic, birds eye chilli, ginger and cook for additional 1 minute.

3. Add the garam masala, turmeric and a few drops of water and cook further for a minute.

4. Add the coconut milk with 200ml of water (Best way is to fill the coconut milk can halfway and pour into the saucepan) add in red lentils. Gently mix thoroughly until well mixed.

5. Cook with the lid on over gently heat for 20 minutes, stirring frequently. Add a few drops of water if too thick.

6. Add the kale once it has cooked for 20 minutes, stirring well and then replace the lid. Continue cooking for additional 5 minutes

7. Meanwhile, cook the buckwheat as instructed in package directions, about 10 minutes) Drain well and serve with the sauce.

Nutrition Information:

kcal: 223
Net carbs: 19 g
Fat: 12g
Fiber: 3 g
Protein: 8g

Spicy Chickpea With Baked Potatoes Stew

Prep time: 10 minutes
Cook time: 60 minutes
Servings: 4-6
INGREDIENTS
(Optional) side salad
(Optional) salt and pepper to taste
2 tbsp of parsley plus extra for garnish
2 yellow peppers, cut into bite-sized pieces (or any color you like)
2 x 400 grams tins chickpeas or kidney beans with the juice
2 tbsp of unsweetened cocoa powder (or cacao)
2 x 400 grams tins chopped tomatoes
Splash of water
2 tbsp of turmeric
2 tbsp of cumin seeds
½ tsp of chilli flakes (Add more if you like it hot)

2 cm grated ginger

4 grated or crushed garlic cloves

2 finely chopped red onions

2 tbsp of olive oil

4-6 baking potatoes, pricked all over

INSTRUCTIONS

1. Heat-up the oven to 200C.

2. Add the potatoes and cook until they are done to your liking. (Mine took 1 hour)

3. Meanwhile, in a large wide saucepan, heat the olive oil, add the onion and gently cook for 5 minutes with the lid on until onions are tender but not browned.

4. Add in the ginger, garlic, chilli and cumin. Reduce to low heat and cook for extra 1 minute. Add in the turmeric and a few drops of water and cook further for a minute. (Keep an eye on it so the pan does not get too dry).

5. Add in cocoa powder, chickpeas with the water, tomatoes and yellow pepper. Cover with a lid and bring to a boil, reduce to low heat then simmer until the sauce is thickened and unctuous, about 45 minutes (do not let it burn!).

6. Add 2 tbsp of parsley, season with salt and pepper (optional). Serve the baked potatoes and top with the stew with a side salad if you wish.

Nutrition Information:

kcal: 320

Net carbs:

Fat: 8g

Fiber: 3 g

Protein: 12 g

Baked Chicken With Walnut

Prep time: 40 minutes

Cook time: 10 minutes

Servings: 1

INGREDIENTS

For the pesto:

Juice 1/2 lemon

1 tbsp of extra virgin olive oil

15 grams of Parmesan

15 grams of walnuts

15 grams of parsley

For the chicken:

1 tsp of balsamic vinegar

100 grams of cherry tomatoes, halved

35 grams of rocket

1 tsp of red wine vinegar

20 grams of red onions, finely sliced

150 grams of skinless chicken breast

INSTRUCTIONS

1. Preheat the oven to 220ºC.

For The Pesto

2. In a food processor, pulse the Parmesan, walnuts, parsley, 1/2 lemon juice olive oil and 1 tbsp water until a smooth paste is formed. Slowly add additional water until your desired consistency is reached.

3 Combine together the remaining lemon juice and 1 tablespoon of the pesto, add the chicken breast, place in the fridge and marinate for 30 minutes or more if you can.

4. Fry the chicken in its marinade over medium-high heat in an ovenproof frying pan for 1 minute on either side.

5. Place the pan in the oven and bake the chicken until cooked through, about 8 minutes.

6. Place the onions in the red wine vinegar and allow marinating for 5-10 minutes, draining off liquid.

7. Once chicken is done, transfer to a plate and spread 1 tablespoon of pesto over chicken and allow the hotness of the chicken melt the pesto. Cover chicken with foil and let sit about 5 minutes before serving.

8. Combine the onion, rocket and tomatoes in a bowl, spread on top the balsamic; Spoon mixture over chicken, spoon the remaining pesto over.

Nutrition Information:

kcal: 300

Fat: 8g

Fiber: 3 g

Protein: 12 g

PORK PAK CHOI

Prep time: 10 minutes

Ready time: 7 minutes

Servings: 4

INGREDIENTS

20 grams large handful of chopped parsley

100 grams of bean sprouts

400 grams of pork mince (10% fat)

200 grams of pak choi or choi sum slices

1 peeled and sliced shallot

100 grams of sliced shiitake mushrooms

1 tbsp of rapeseed oil

(5cm) 1 thumb of fresh grated ginger

1 crushed clove garlic

1 tbsp of soy sauce

1 tsp of brown sugar

1 tbsp of tomato purée

1 tbsp of rice wine

125 ml of chicken stock

1 tbsp of water

1 tbsp of corn flour

400 grams of firm tofu, cut into large cubes

INSTRUCTIONS

1. Place the tofu between kitchen papers and set aside.

2. Combine water and corn flour together in a small bowl and remove all lumps. Pour in the rice wine, chicken stock, tomato purée, soy sauce and brown sugar. Add the crushed ginger and garlic and stir together.

3. Heat the oil in a large frying pan or a wok over high heat. Add in the mushrooms and cook stirring continuously for 2 to 3 minutes until cooked. Remove the mushrooms and place aside.

4. Place tofu into the frying pan and cook stirring constantly until all sides are golden. Remove from pan and set aside.

5. Add the pak choi and shallot to the pan; cook stirring constantly about 2 minutes.

6. Add the pork mince, stirring constantly for few minutes until rich and golden, then add the sauce, turn heat down a bit and simmer for a minute or two until bubbly around the meat.

7. Add in the tofu, mushrooms and bean sprouts into the pan and cook until heated through. Remove and stir in the parsley. Enjoy!

Nutrition Information:

kcal: 377

Net carbs: 12

Fat: 25g

Fiber: 2.6 g

Protein: 41 g

Sirtfood Pasta Salad

Servings: 1

INGREDIENTS

20 grams of pine nuts
1 tbsp of extra virgin olive oil
10 olives
1/2 diced avocado
8 cherry tomatoes, halved
Small handful of basil leaves
A large handful of rocket
50 grams of buckwheat pasta (cooked according to the packet instructions)

INSTRUCTIONS

1. Cook the buckwheat noodles according to the packet instructions.
2. Combine together the cooked pasta, olive oil, olives, diced avocado, basil leaves, tomatoes and rocket in a bowl. Serve noodles on a plate and spread the pine nuts over top.

Nutrition Information:
kcal: 290; Net carbs: 7.2; Fat: 31.52g; Protein: 3.92 g

Beef Red Onion Potatoes Burgers

Prep time: 15 minutes

Ready time: 30 minutes

Servings: 1

INGREDIENTS

(Optional) 1 gherkin

10 grams of rocket

30 grams of tomato, sliced

150 grams of red onion, sliced into rings

10 grams of sliced or grated Cheddar cheese

1 unpeeled garlic clove

1 tsp of dried rosemary

1 tsp of olive oil

150 grams of sweet potatoes, peel and cut into 1cm- thick chips

1 tsp of olive oil

1 tsp of finely chopped parsley

15 grams of finely chopped red onion

125 grams of lean minced beef (5% fat)

INSTRUCTIONS

1. Preheat the oven to 450 f.

2. Toss sweet potato chips with the oil, garlic clove and rosemary. Add to the baking pan and roast in the oven until nice and crispy, about 30 minutes.

3. Mix the minced beef with parsley and onion. Mold using your hands into an even patty or use a pastry cutters and mold, if you have one.

4. Heat the olive oil over medium heat in a hot frying pan; add onion rings towards one side of the frying pan and the burger over the other. Cook onion rings to your liking and burger for about 6 minutes per side until burger is cooked through.

5. Top the burger with the red onion and cheese, transfer to the preheated oven until cheese is melted. Remove from the oven and top with the tomato, gherkin and rocket. Serve along the fries.

Nutrition Information:

kcal: 406

Net carbs: 35g

Fat: 17g

Fiber: 5.5 g

Protein: 32.17 g

Braised Carrots Puy Lentils

Prep time: 40 minutes

Cook time: 60 minutes

Servings: 1

INGREDIENTS

20 grams of rocket

1 tbsp of parsley, chopped

50 grams of kale, roughly chopped

220 ml of vegetable stock

75 grams of puy lentils

1 tsp of thyme (dry or fresh)

1 tsp of paprika

40 grams of carrots, peeled and thinly sliced

40 grams of thinly sliced Celery

1 finely chopped garlic clove

40 grams of thinly sliced red onion

2 tsp of extra virgin olive oil

8 cherry tomatoes, halved

INSTRUCTIONS

1. Heat the oven to 120 C

2. Roast the tomatoes in the oven in a small baking pan for 35–45 minutes.

3. Heat 1 teaspoon of the olive oil over low–medium heat in a saucepan. Add the onion, celery, garlic, and carrot slices and cook for 1 to 2 minutes until tender. Add the thyme and paprika and cook for extra 1 minute.

4. Add lentils and Vegetable stock into the pan, and bring to the boil. Turn heat down and simmer with the lid on for 20 minutes. Add a splash of water if needed and make sure you stir 5-7 minutes intervals.

5. Add in kale and keep cooking for another 10 minutes. Stir in the roasted tomatoes and parsley. Serve along the rocket and drizzle top with the remaining olive oil.

Nutrition Information:
kcal: 283
Net carbs: 45g
Fat: 17g
Fiber: 9.6g
Protein: 5.71 g

Sweet Potato Hummus With Bean Falafel And Couscous

Prep time: 30 minutes
Cook time: 30 minutes
Servings: 4
INGREDIENTS
For the hummus
1 tbsp of olive oil
1 crushed garlic clove
Juice of 1 lemon
3 tbsp of tahini
350 grams of sweet potato
For The falafel
3 tbsp of olive oil, plus more for greasing
Small handful of coriander, roughly chopped
Small handful of parsley, roughly chopped
125 grams of self-rising flour
1 medium egg
2 tsp of ground cumin

3 crushed garlic cloves

1 roughly chopped red onion

1/2 green chilli, remove seeds and chopped finely

400 grams of tin mixed beans, drained and rinsed

For the herby couscous

150 ml hot of vegetable stock

150 grams of couscous

INSTRUCTIONS

1 Heat-up the oven to 395 f. Line your baking tray with parchment paper.

2. Scrub the potatoes under running tap and cut into small pieces. Mix ½ tsp olive oil and sweet potato with a generous seasoning in a large roasting tin. Cook until softened about 20 minutes. Set aside until ready to use. (Do not turn off the oven).

How To Make The Falafel

2 Meanwhile, blend the entire falafel ingredients with a generous seasoning (with the exception of oil) in a blender until partially smooth. Chill in the refrigerator for 30 minutes to firm up.

3. Heat 3 tablespoons of the oil over medium-high heat in a large skillet. Use two grease spoons to drop the falafel mixture, about the size of a walnut into the hot oil. You can do in batches. Cook for about 8 minutes, stirring periodically until golden brown.

4. Place falafel balls into the prepared baking tray and cook in the oven for 15 minutes.

4 While falafel balls are cooking, place the couscous along with hot vegetable stock in a large heatproof dish. Cover with cling wrap and let sit about 5 minutes. Fluff up the couscous using a fork, add the cherries/sultanas, herbs, lemon juice with the seasoning and mix well.

5 Combine the cooked potatoes, remaining half tablespoon of oil, lemon juice, tahini, garlic and water into the blender until smooth. Taste and adjust seasoning if needed. Serve in 4 bowls and add the falafel over top along with the hummus.

Baked Salmon

Prep time: 15-20 minutes
Cook time: 10 minutes
Servings: 1

INGREDIENTS

1/4 Juice of a lemon
1 tsp of ground turmeric
1 tsp of extra virgin olive oil
125-150 grams of skinned salmon

For the spicy celery

1 tbsp of chopped parsley
100 ml vegetable or chicken stock
130 grams of tomato, cut into 8 wedges
1 tsp of mild curry powder
150 grams of celery, cut into 2 cm lengths
1 finely chopped Bird's eye chilli
1 cm finely chopped fresh ginger
1 Garlic clove, finely chopped
60 grams of tinned green lentils
40 grams of red onion, finely chopped
1 tsp of extra virgin olive oil

INSTRUCTIONS
1. Preheat your oven to 200C / gas mark 6.
For the spicy celery
2. Heat the olive oil over medium–low heat in a hot frying pan; add the garlic, onion, chilli, ginger and celery. Gently sauté for about 2–3 minutes, then pour in the curry powder and sauté for another minute.
3. Add the tomatoes, lentils and vegetable or chicken stock and gently simmer for 7-10 minutes.
4. Meanwhile, mix the lemon juice, oil and turmeric and rub all over the salmon.
5. Place seasoned salmon onto a baking tray and cook in the preheated oven for 8–10 minutes. Stir the parsley into the celery mixture and serve over the salmon.

Nutrition Information:
kcal: 340
Net carbs: 25g
Fat: 11.9g
Fiber: 7.5g
Protein: 41 g

Buckwheat Noodles With Stir-Fry Prawn

Prep time: 10 minutes

Cook time: 10 minutes

Servings: 1

INGREDIENTS

5g lovage or celery leaves

100 ml of chicken stock

50 g roughly chopped kale

75g chopped green beans

40g trimmed and sliced celery

20g sliced red onions

1 tsp of finely chopped fresh ginger

1 finely chopped bird's eye chilli

1 finely chopped garlic clove

75g of soba buckwheat noodles

2 tsp of extra virgin olive oil

2 tsp soy sauce or soy sauce

150g of shelled raw king prawns, deveined

INSTRUCTIONS

1. Heat 1 tsp of the oil and 1 tsp. of the soy sauce over high heat in a frying pan, add prawns and cook about 2–3 minutes. Set prawns aside in a plate. Prepare the pan for another use.

2. Cook the buckwheat noodles the way instructed in package instruction. Drain and set aside.

3. Meanwhile, heat the remaining oil over medium–high and fry the red onion, garlic, ginger, chilli, celery and kale and beans for 2–3 minutes. Add in the chicken stock and bring to a boil, simmer for 1 t0 2 minute until the vegetables are soft but still firm to the bite.

4. Add buckwheat noodles, prawns, noodles and lovage to the pan, bring to a boil. Turn heat off and serve.

Buckwheat Pasta With Prawn And Arrabbiata Sauce

Prep time: 35 minutes
Cook time: 30 to 40 minutes
Servings: 1

INGREDIENTS

1 tbsp of extra virgin olive oil
65 grams of buckwheat pasta
125 to 150 grams of raw or cooked prawns (for best result use king prawns)

For arrabbiata sauce

1 tbsp of chopped parsley
400 grams of tinned chopped tomatoes
(Optional) 2 tbsp of white wine
1 tsp of extra virgin olive oil
1 tsp of dried mixed herbs
1 finely chopped Bird's eye chilli
30 grams of celery, finely chopped
1 finely chopped garlic clove
40 grams of red onion, finely chopped

INSTRUCTIONS

1. Heat the olive oil in a frying pan over medium–low heat. Add the onion, celery garlic, dried herbs and chilli and sauté for 1–2 minutes. Increase to medium heat, add white wine (if using) and cook for one minute. Add the tomatoes and simmer for 20–30 minutes over a medium–low heat or until desired consistency is reached.
2. Meanwhile, cook the pasta as instructed in package directions, drain. Add 1 tbsp of olive oil to cooked pasta, toss to coat. Set aside in pan.
3. Add raw prawns into the sauce and cook for additional 3 to 4 minutes or until cooked and color is pink and opaque. Add in the parsley.
4. Add the earlier set aside pasta into the sauce, gently mix but thoroughly, serve and enjoy.

Notes:
If you are using cooked prawns, you do not need to cook for the extra 3-4 minutes, just add cooked prawns along with the parsley and bring to a boil.

Nutrition Information:
kcal: 305
Net carbs: 25g
Fat: 11.15g
Fiber: 6g
Protein: 33.8 g

Baked Mackerel Fillets With Potatoes

Prep time: 5 minutes

Cook time: 25 minutes

Servings: 4

INGREDIENTS

1/4 pint of vegetable stock

1 tbsp of olive oil

7-ounces of cherry tomatoes

2-ounces of pitted black olives

11-ounces of mackerel fillets

1 lemon

2 sweet potatoes, chopped

2 leeks, chopped

INSTRUCTIONS

1. Heat-up the oven to 375 F. Place the leeks and sweet potatoes in a roasting pan. Add the stock and drizzle with 1 tablespoon of olive oil.

2. Place pan in the oven and roast for 15-20 minutes until potatoes are soft. Add the cherry tomatoes, mackerel fillets and black olives. Top with a squeeze of lemon juice and roast for extra 10 minutes.

Nutrition Information:

kcal: 230; Net carbs: 21g; Fat: 7.4g; Fiber: 4g; Protein: 18.22 g

Buckwheat Noodles With Chicken Miso Dressing

Prep time: 15 minutes

Cook time: 15 minutes

Servings: 2

INGREDIENTS

For The Noodles

2-3 tbsp of soy sauce

2 large finely diced garlic cloves

1 long thinly sliced red chilli, (leave the seeds if you like it hot)

1 sliced or diced medium chicken breast (free-range chicken)

1 finely diced brown onion

1 tsp of coconut oil or ghee

3-4 sliced shiitake mushrooms

5 ounces of 100% buckwheat noodles (150 g)

2-3 handfuls of kale leaves (detached from the stem and roughly chopped)

For The Dressing

1 tbsp of lemon or lime juice

1 tbsp of extra-virgin olive oil

1 tbsp of soy sauce

1½ tbsp of fresh organic miso

(Optional) 1 tsp of sesame oil

INSTRUCTIONS

1. Cook kale for about 1 minute in boiling water in a medium saucepan or until a bit wilted. Remove kale and bring water back to a boil. Add buckwheat noodles and cook as instructed in the package directions. Rinse the cooked noodles under cold water, drain and set aside.

2. Meanwhile, add about a teaspoon of coconut oil or ghee to a frying pan and fry the mushrooms until lightly browned on both sides, about 2-3 minutes. Season with salt and set aside.

3. Heat more ghee or coconut oil or in the same pan, over medium-high heat. Add onion and chilli and stir-fry for 2-3 minutes.

4. Add pieces of chicken and cook over medium heat for 5 minutes, stirring periodically, then add soy sauce, little drops of water and garlic. Cook for additional 2-3 minutes, stirring constantly.

5. Lastly, add the noodles and kale, toss with the chicken to heat up.

For The Miso Dressing

6. Mix together the entire miso dressing ingredients in a bowl. Drizzle dressing on top the noodles and chicken just towards the final cooking time.

Nutrition Information:

kcal: 420

Net carbs: 25g

Fat: 21g

Fiber: 4.6g

Protein: 38 g

Strawberry Dates Avocado Buckwheat Tabouleh

Prep time: 10 minutes

Cook time: 10 minutes

Servings: 1

INGREDIENTS

30 grams of rocket

Half lemon juice

1 tbsp of extra virgin olive oil

100 grams of hulled strawberries, sliced

30 grams of finely chopped parsley

1 tbsp of finely chopped capers

25 grams pitted Medjool dates

20 grams of finely chopped red onion

65 grams of finely chopped tomato

80 grams of finely chopped avocado

1 tbsp of ground turmeric

50 grams of buckwheat

INSTRUCTIONS

1. Cook the buckwheat noodles along with the turmeric the way instructed in package instruction. (Takes about 5-8 minutes) Drain and set aside to cool.
2. Mix the cooled buckwheat with parsley, red onion, tomato, avocado, dates and capers.
3. Gently stir the strawberries, lemon juice and oil into the salad. Serve mixture on a bed of rocket.

Nutrition Information:
kcal: 390
Net carbs: 30g
Fat: 19g
Fiber: 15g
Protein: 8 g

Tofu Curry And Kale, Edamame

Prep time: 5 minutes
Ready time: 45 minutes
Servings: 4

INGREDIENTS

1 tbsp of rapeseed oil
1 chopped large onion
4 peeled and grated cloves garlic
1 large thumb (7cm) fresh ginger, peeled and grated
1 red chilli, seed removed and thinly sliced
1/2 tsp of ground turmeric
1/4 tsp of cayenne pepper
1 tsp of paprika
1/2 tsp of ground cumin
1 tsp of salt
250 grams of dried red lentils
1 liter of hot water
50 grams of frozen soya edamame beans
200 grams of firm tofu, chopped into cubes
2 roughly chopped tomatoes
Juice of 1 lime
200 grams of kale leaves, remove stalks and tear leaves apart

INSTRUCTIONS

1. Heat the oil over low-medium heat in a heavy-bottomed pan. Sauté the onion oil for 5 minutes, add in grated garlic, chilli and grated ginger and cook for another 2 minutes.
2. Add the paprika, cayenne, cumin, turmeric and salt. Stir thoroughly, then add the red lentils, stir to combine.
3. Add hot water and bring mixture to a simmer for about 10 minutes. Turn heat down and cook until the curry has thickened, about 20 to 30 minutes.
4. Add the tomatoes, tofu and soya beans and keep cooking for another 5 minutes. Add the kale leaves and lime juice and cook until the kale is soft.

Nutrition Information:

kcal: 342, Net carbs: 29g
Fat: 8.52g, Fiber: 10g, Protein: 23

Salmon Salad With Creamy Mayo Dressing

Prep time: 5 minutes

Cook time: 18 minutes

Servings: 1

INGREDIENTS

(10 grams) 1 small handful of roughly chopped parsley

2 spring onions, trimmed and sliced

50 grams of cucumber, 5cm piece cut into chunks

2 trimmed and thinly sliced radishes

40 grams of young spinach leaves

40 grams of mixed salad leaves

130 grams (1) salmon fillet

For the dressing:

Salt and freshly ground black pepper

2 finely chopped leaves mint

1 tbsp of rice vinegar

1 tbsp of natural yogurt

1 tsp of low-fat mayonnaise

INSTRUCTIONS

1 Heat-up your oven to 200°C.

2 Arrange the salmon fillet skin side down over a baking pan, place in the oven and bake until salmon fillet is just cooked through, about 16–18. Remove skin using a fish slice and set aside.

3. Combine the rice wine vinegar, yogurt, mayonnaise, salt, mint leaves and pepper together in a small bowl, let stand at least 5 minutes to mend flavors.

4. Place the spinach and salad leaves onto a serving plate; top with spring onions, radishes, parsley and cucumber. Flake the cooked salmon with a fork over the salad and drizzle the dressing on top.

Nutrition Information: Mixed Salad leaves excluded

kcal: 250

Net carbs: 6g

Fat: 11g

Fiber: 5g

Protein: 31 g

Chicken & Kale Curry Sirtfood

Prep time: 20 minutes

Ready time: 60 minutes

Servings: 4

INGREDIENTS

175 grams of tinned chopped tomatoes

500 ml of boiling water

1 chicken stock pot

200 ml of tinned light coconut milk

1 tin chopped tomato

2 cardamom pods

1 tbsp of curry powder

1 tbsp of freshly chopped ginger

2 finely chopped birds eye chilli

3 crushed garlic cloves

2 diced red onions

2 tbsp of ground tumeric

1 tbsp of olive oil

400 grams of skinless and boneless chicken thighs

INSTRUCTIONS

1. Arrange the chicken in a ceramic-lined or glass bowl (Make sure it's non-metallic), add 1 tablespoon of the turmeric and 1 teaspoon of the olive oil. Mix mixture together with a spoon and leave for 30 minutes to marinate.

2. Fry the chicken for 4-5 minutes in a frying pan over medium heat until browned on all sides and cooked through. Set aside.

3. Heat the reserved oil in the frying pan over medium heat; add the onion, ginger   garlic and chilli and sauté for 10 minutes until soft. (Keep the kitchen ventilated)

4. Add additional tbsp. of turmeric and curry powder and cook for extra 1-2 minutes.

Add the coconut milk, tomatoes, cardamom pods and chicken stock. Simmer for about 30 minutes until sauce has reduced a little.

5. Add in the chicken and kale. Cook until kale is tender and chicken is warmed. Garnish with chopped coriander and serve over buckwheat or rice.

 Nutrition Information:

kcal: 313;Net carbs: 9g;Fat: 21g; Protein: 21 g

SIRTFOOD SOUP RECIPES

Cannellini Bean And Kale Soup

Prep time: 15 minutes
Cook time: 30 minutes
Servings: 2-3

INGREDIENTS

1/4 lemon juice
1 1/2 cups of loosely packed kale (stemmed and roughly chopped)
19 ounces can of cannellini beans, rinsed and drained or 4 cups cooked
1/8 to 1/4 tsp of red chili flakes
1/2 tsp of sea salt
1/4 tsp of black pepper
1/2 tsp of smoked sweet paprika
1.5 sprigs fresh thyme, de-stemmed
1/2 bay leaf
2.5 cups of low-sodium vegetable stock
1 medium carrots, peeled and chopped
1 sliced celery stalks
1 minced cloves garlic
1/2 finely chopped shallot
1/2 tbsp of extra virgin olive oil

INSTRUCTIONS

1. Heat the oil in a large pot over medium heat. Add garlic and shallot and cook for 1-2 minutes until soft and fragrant. Add the carrots and celery, cook stirring frequently for 3 minutes.
2. Add the bay leaf, stock, paprika, thyme, cannellini beans, salt, chili flakes, and black pepper and bring to a simmer. Cover with a lid and reduce to low-medium heat, simmer, stirring halfway through until the vegetables are soft, about 25 to 30 minutes. Discard bay leaf.
3. Scoop about four cups of the liquid into a high-powered blender and blend for 10 seconds. Transfer the puréed liquid back to the pot. Stir in lemon juice and kale and simmer for extra 5 minutes. Serve soup in bowls and enjoy.
4. Leftovers can be stored in the fridge in an airtight container for up to 6 days or 1 month in the freezer.

Nutrition Information:
kcal: 193

Net carbs: 27g
Fat: 3g
Fiber: 10g
Protein: 12 g

Tofu Buckwheat Soba Noodles Carrots And Kale Soup

Prep time: 15 minutes

Cook time: 20 minutes

Servings: 2

INGREDIENTS

Salt and freshly ground black pepper

1 handful of chopped kale

2-3 finely chopped scallions

2 garlic cloves, minced

2 medium carrots, chop into small pieces

3 cups of vegetable broth

75 grams soba (buckwheat) noodles

Some chili flakes

1 organic lime or lemon

1 tbsp of oil

200 grams of tofu

INSTRUCTIONS

1. Place the tofu between two sheets of paper towel to dry off; cut into cubes. Place the tofu in a bowl and season with some chili flakes, salt and pepper; toss to coat.

2. Heat the oil over medium heat, add the tofu and fry until all sides are golden brown. Sprinkle some lime zest over.

3. Add the vegetable broth to a pot and bring to a boil. Add in the chopped carrots and cook until tender. Remove carrots from the soup with a slotted spoon; Season with lots of pepper and salt.

4. Meanwhile, cook the noodles as directed in package instructions.

Add the minced garlic into 2 serving bowls along with the scallions; add chopped kale, cooked carrots, tofu, noodles and kale. Pour soup over and serve with the lime wedges.

Carrots Lentil Rosemary Soup

Prep time: 20 minutes
Cook time: 20 minutes
Servings: 6

INGREDIENTS

Juice of 1/2 small lemon
1/2 tsp of salt
1/2 bay leaf
1 sprigs fresh rosemary
3 sprigs of fresh thyme or 1/2 tsp of dried thyme leaves
1/2 cups of dry uncooked brown lentils
2.5 cups of stock
1 finely chopped ribs celery
1 finely chopped carrots
1 tbsp of tomato paste
2 minced cloves garlic
1/2 diced onion
1 1/2 tbsp of olive oil

INSTRUCTIONS

1. Sauté onion in hot oil in a medium pot over medium heat for 5-7 minutes until tender and translucent. Stir in the garlic and cook for another minute.
2. Pour in the tomato paste; stir well until coated in the mixture, cook about 2-3 minutes.
3. Add the celery, carrots, rosemary, lentils, stock, thyme, bay leaf and salt.
Cover with a lid and bring to a gentle boil. Turn heat down and cook until lentils are tender as desire, about 35-40 minutes.

4. Remove bay leaves and herbs, pour the mixture into a high-powered blender and puree. Stir in lemon juice. Enjoy!

Nutrition Information:

kcal: 210

Net carbs: 25g

Fat: 7.4g

Fiber: 11g

Protein: 9 g

Sirtfood Vegetable Soup

Prep time: 15 minutes

Cook time: 40 minutes

Servings: 6

INGREDIENTS

15 ounces can of kidney beans (drained and rinsed)

4 cups of vegetable stock

15 ounces can of diced tomatoes (plus the juices)

1 bay leaf

1/2 tsp of salt

1 tsp of oregano

1 cup of zucchini, cut into about 1 inch pieces

1 cup of cauliflower florets, cut into about 1 inch pieces

1 tsp of basil

2 peeled and sliced celery ribs

2 sliced carrots

3 minced cloves garlic

1 chopped red onion

1 tbsp of olive oil

INSTRUCTIONS

1. In a large pot, heat the olive oil over medium heat. Sauté the onion in hot oil for 5-7 minutes until onion is tender. Place the garlic and cook further for one minute.

2. Add the carrots, zucchini, cauliflower, basil, oregano, celery, diced tomatoes, vegetable stock, bay leaf and salt. Give it a good stir and cover with a lid, bring mixture to a boil.

3. Reduce heat and let it simmer for about 30 minutes or until veggies are soft.

4. Add in the kidney beans, stir and remove bay leaf before serving.

Nutrition Information:

kcal: 159

Net carbs: 20g

Fat: 3g

Fiber: 7g

Protein: 7 g

SALAD RECIPES

Walnuts Avocado Salad

Ready time: 8 minutes

Servings: 1

INGREDIENTS

1/4 cup of chopped parsley

1/4 lemon juice

1 tbsp of extra virgin olive oil

1 large Medjool date, pitted and chopped

1 tbsp of capers

1/8 cups of chopped walnuts

1/8 cup of sliced red onion

1/2 cup of celery including leaves, sliced

1/2 cup of avocado, peeled, stoned, and sliced

100 grams of smoked salmon slices (3 1/2 oz)

50 grams of endive leaves (1 3/4 oz)

50 grams of arugula (1 3/4 oz)

INSTRUCTIONS

1. Place the endive leaves, parsley, celery leaves and arugula in a large bowl or plate.

2. Mix together the remaining ingredients and serve over of the leaves.

Poached Pear Salad With Dijon Vinegar Dressing

Ready time: 15 minutes

Servings: 1

INGREDIENTS

For The Dressing

75 ml olive oil

75 ml walnut oil

1 tbsp of red wine vinegar

1 tbsp of Dijon mustard

Freshly ground Pepper to taste

Salt to taste

FOR THE SALAD

200 grams of Gorgonzola cheese, slice finely

Few rocket leaves

100 grams of Walnuts

2 Ripe pears (peeled and core) cut into quarters

2 Bay leaves

Small bunch of thyme

40 grams of caster sugar

180 ml of red wine

INSTRUCTIONS

1. Bring the wine to a boil in a saucepan along with the bay leaves, sugar and thyme. simmer over medium-low heat.

2. Add the pear into the simmering liquid and poach for 10 minutes. Remove pan from heat and set aside to cool pears in poaching liquid.

3. In a bowl, whisk together the mustard, salt, vinegar, and pepper until well whisk; slowly steam in the oil and whisking as you add.

4. Arrange salad ingredients on a serving plate and drizzle with the dressing.

Steak Arugula Strawberry Salad

Prep time: 10 minutes

Cook time: 15 minutes

Servings: 4

INGREDIENTS

Steak:

1/2 tbsp extra virgin olive oil

Montreal steak seasoning

2 Beef tenderloin steaks

Salad:

1/8 cup of slivered walnuts

1/4 cup of crumbled feta cheese

1/2 cup of sliced strawberries

1/2 cup blueberries

1/2 cup of raspberries

3 cups of arugula

Balsamic Vinaigrette

Salt and pepper

1/4 tsp of Dijon mustard

1 1/2 tsp of sugar

1/8 cup of olive oil

1/8 cup of balsamic vinegar

INSTRUCTIONS

Steak:

1. Run the Montreal steak seasoning all over the steak and let sit for 5-10 minutes.

2. Heat oil over medium high heat in a cast-iron skillet. Once it's simmering, add in the steak and cook about 5-7 minutes; flip and cook the other side for 3-4 minutes or until its cooked the way you like your meet.

3. Set steak aside in a plate and let cool for 5 minutes before slicing into strips.

Salad

4. In a large bowl, combine together the salad ingredients.

5. In a small shaker, add together the all vinaigrette ingredients and shake until well mixed. Pour dressing over salad and toss to evenly coat.

To Serve

Divide the salad between 2 bowls, and top with steak.

Notes:

You can keep the dressing for up to one week in the fridge.

Nutrition Information:

kcal: 506

Net carbs: 17g

Fat: 37g

Fiber: 5g

Protein: 23 g

Super Fruit Salad

Ready time: 10 minutes

Servings: 1

INGREDIENTS

10 blueberries

10 red seedless grapes

1 apple, cored and chopped roughly

1 orange, halved

1 tsp of honey

½ cup of freshly made matcha green tea

INSTRUCTIONS

1. Combine 1/2 cup green tea with the honey and stir until dissolved, Squeeze in half of the orange into the green tea mix. Leave to cool.

2. Chop the second orange half into pieces and transfer into a bowl. Add in the blueberries, chopped apple and grapes. Pour the cooled tea on top the salad mix and allow to soak a little before serving.

Nutrition Information:
kcal: 200
Net carbs: 40g
Fat: 1g
Fiber: 5g
Protein: 2 g

Sirtfood Salmon Lentils Salad
Prep time: 10 minutes
Cook time: 0 minutes
Servings: 1
INGREDIENTS
20 grams of sliced red onion
40 grams of sliced celery
10 grams of chopped lovage
10 grams of chopped parsley
Juice of 1/4 of a lemon
1 tbsp of extra virgin olive oil
1 large Medjool date, remove pit and chopped
1 tbsp of capers
15 grams of chopped walnuts
80 grams of avocado, peeled, pitted and sliced
100g tinned green lentils or cooked Puy lentils
50 grams of chicory leaves
50 grams of rocket
INSTRUCTIONS
1. On a large plate, add the salad leaves. Mix together the remaining ingredients and spread mixture over leaves to serve.

Nutrition Information:

kcal: 400

Net carbs: 20g

Fat: 25g

Fiber: 14g

Protein: 10 g

Blueberry Kale Salad With Ginger Lime Dressing

Prep time: 10 minutes

Cook time: 60 minutes

Servings: 4

INGREDIENTS

3 tbsp of white wine vinegar

1 tbsp of honey

2 tbsp of finely chopped ginger, crystallized

3 tbsp of lime juice

Salt and pepper to taste

Salad:

1/4 cup of slivered walnuts toasted

1/2-3/4 cup of fresh blueberries

1/3 thinly sliced red onion

8 cups of kale, de-stemmed and chopped into pieces

INSTRUCTIONS

1. Combine together the entire dressing ingredients in a medium bowl until well mixed.

2. Add sliced onion chopped kale, toss to coat. Leave to marinate for about 1-4 hours, depending on how much time you have, tossing periodically. This is an important step to remove the bitterness from the kale.

3. Add toasted walnuts and blueberries. Toss to coat.

Nutrition Information:

kcal: 91

Net carbs: 10g

Fat: 3.69g

Fiber: 3g

Protein: 3g

Fancy Chicken Salad

Prep time: 1 minute

Cook time: 10 minutes

Servings: 1

INGREDIENTS

1 bird's eye chilli

20 grams of diced red onion

1 finely chopped medjool date

6 finely chopped Walnut halves

100 grams of cooked chicken breast, chopped into bite-sized chunks

1/2 tsp of mild curry powder

1 tsp of ground turmeric

1 tsp of chopped Coriander

Juice of 1/4 of a lemon

75 grams of natural yoghurt

40 grams of rocket

INSTRUCTIONS

1. In a bowl, mix together the lemon juice, yoghurt, spices and coriander. Mix in the remaining ingredients until well blended. Serve over bed of the rocket.

Nutrition Information: natural yoghurt not included

kcal: 340

Net carbs: 22g

Fat: 13g

Fiber: 5g
Protein: 36g

Olive, Tomato, Yellow Pepper, Red Onion, Cucumber Slices And Feta Skewers

Prep time: 5 minutes
Ready time: 10 minutes
Servings: 2

INGREDIENTS

100 grams of feta, cut into 8 cubes
100 grams of cucumber, cut in quarters and halved
Half red onion, cut in half and sliced into 8 pieces
1 yellow pepper (or any color you like) cut into 8 squares
8 cherry tomatoes
8 large black olives
2 wooden skewers, soaked for 30 minutes in water before use
For the dressing:
½ crushed clove garlic
1 tsp of balsamic vinegar

½ lemon Juice

Few finely chopped basil leaves (or ½ tsp of dried mixed herbs)

1 tbsp of extra virgin olive oil

Few leaves finely chopped oregano (Skip this if using dried mixed herbs)

Freshly ground black pepper

Salt to taste

INSTRUCTIONS

1. Pierce each skewer through the olive, tomato, yellow pepper, red onion, cucumber slices and feta. Repeat a second time.

2. Combine the dressing ingredients in a sealable container and mix thoroughly. Pour dressing over the skewers.

Nutrition Information:

kcal: 228

Net carbs: 13g

Fat: 15g

Fiber: 3g

Protein: 8.7g

Sesame Soy Chicken Salad

Prep time: 10 minutes

Ready time: 12 minutes

Servings: 2

INGREDIENTS

INGREDIENTS

150 grams of cooked chicken, shredded

Large handful of chopped parsley (20g)

½ finely sliced red onion

60 grams of pak choi, very finely shredded

100 grams of roughly chopped baby kale

1 peeled cucumber, slice in half lengthwise, remove seed and cut into slices

1 tbsp of sesame seeds

For the dressing:

2 tsp of soy sauce

1 tsp of clear honey

Juice of 1 lime

1 tsp of sesame oil

1 tbsp of extra virgin olive oil

INSTRUCTIONS

1. Clean your frying pan well and make sure it's dry, toast the sesame seeds for 2 minutes in the pan until fragrant and lightly browned. Set aside in a plate to cool.

To Make The Dressing

2. Mix together the soy sauce, olive oil, lime juice, sesame oil and honey in a small bowl.

3. Place the kale, cucumber, parsley, red onion and pak choi in a large bowl and mix gently. Pour dressing over salad and mix together.

4. Serve the salad in two different plates and add shredded chicken on top. Just before serving, sprinkle with sesame seeds.

Nutrition Information:
kcal: 304 cals

Salmon Chicory Rocket Super Salad
Ready time: 10
Serves: 1
INGREDIENTS
10 grams of chopped lovage or celery leaves
10 grams of chopped parsley
Juice ¼ lemon
1 tbsp of extra-virgin olive oil
1 large medjool date, pitted and chopped
1 tbsp of capers
15 grams of chopped walnuts
20 grams of sliced red onion
40 grams of sliced celery
80 grams of avocado, peeled, sliced
100 grams of smoked salmon slices or cooked chicken breast
50 grams of chicory leaves
50 grams of rocket
INSTRUCTIONS
1. On a large plate, place the salad leaves. Mix together the remaining ingredients and spread mixture over leaves to serve.

Nutrition Information:
kcal: 300
Net carbs: 30g
Fat: 21g
Fiber: 10g
Protein: 20g

Fresh Chopped Salad With Vinegar

Prep time: 20 minutes

Cook time: 20 minutes

Servings: 8

INGREDIENTS

1/2 cup of fresh parsley, coarsely chopped

1/2 cup of Kalamata olives, pitted and chopped coarsely

Freshly ground pepper

4 medium seeded and diced tomatoes

2 tablespoon of white-wine vinegar

1/2 cup of chopped scallions

1/2 teaspoon salt

2 cup of diced seedless cucumber

4 tablespoons of extra-virgin olive oil

INSTRUCTIONS

1. Combine all the entire ingredients in a medium bowl; carefully toss to combine finely. Serve within an hour.

Nutrition Information:

kcal: 113

Net carbs: 5g

Fat: 10g

Protein: 1g

King Prawns Prawn Parcels

Prep time: 15 minutes

Cook time: 10-15 minutes

Servings: 2

INGREDIENTS

2 lemon slices

50 ml of vegetable stock

1 tsp of garlic crushed

300 grams of king prawns raw or cooked

2 thinly sliced broccoli florets

1 stick celery

1 courgette

1 carrot, peeled

(Optional) fresh dill

INSTRUCTIONS

1. Heat your oven to 180C or 160C fan

2. Shave the carrot, courgette and celery into ribbons with veggie peeler and set aside.

3. Arrange two pieces of tin foil, (large enough to hold your vegetables) add a smaller piece of greaseproof paper on top each tin foil. Curl up edges so the filling can hold.

4. Add half of the veggies over each piece of paper; add the prawns and a slice of lemon.

5. Mix vegetable stock with garlic and add on top the veggies. Sprinkle top with dill if using. Seal the foil and transfer to the baking sheet.

6. Place baking sheet in the oven and bake until vegetables are soft, about 10-15 minutes. Remove foil and serve.

Nutrition Information:
kcal: 204
Net carbs: 4g
Fat: 3g
Fiber: 10g
Protein: 36g

SIRTFOOD SNACKS AND BITES

Buckwheat Feta Apple Galettes

Prep time: 1-2 hours

Cook time: 30 minutes

Servings: 4

INGREDIENTS

For The Galettes

Salt and freshly ground black pepper

Dash of olive oil

1 tbsp of ghee

50 grams of melted butter

1 free-range egg

100 grams of buckwheat flour

For The Filling:

Squeeze lemon juice

Freshly ground black pepper, to taste

Pinch sea salt flakes

2 green apples, peeled and cored (chopped into small chunks, about 1¼ inch)

2 large thinly sliced red onions

2 tbsp of butter

200 grams of feta to serve

70 grams of bag arugula, washed and dried, to serve

INSTRUCTIONS

1. Heat your oven to 200C. Line a baking tray with baking parchment.

2. In a mixing bowl, sift the flour and then season with pepper and salt. Add the egg and slowly stream in about 300 ml of water, whisking until a smooth thick batter is formed. Set aside for 60 minutes.

3. While the batter is resting, melt the butter over medium heat in a frying pan. Add in the onions slices and sauté until tender but not colored, about 4-5 minutes.

4. Add chunk of apples and keep cooking for 10-15 minutes, stirring frequently until apples are tender and beginning to brown; Season with lemon juice, salt and pepper. Set aside and keep warm.

5. Once the batter has rested for an hour, mix in the melted butter until fully mixed.

6. In a heavy-based or ceramic frying pan, heat the olive oil and ghee over medium-high heat. Add one tablespoonful of the batter into the frying pan and swirl around so that the batter spreads and cover the bottom of the pan. Cook for 2 to 3 minutes or until golden-brown under, flip and cook for one minute more. Remove and keep warn while you prepare the remaining batter. (I placed mine in the oven to keep warm)

7. In the middle of each galette, add a handful of arugula leaves. Evenly spoon the apple mix over each galettes and crumble the feta over top. Fold edges to form a square.

8. Place galettes on a parchment paper lined baking tray and bake for 6-7 minutes in the oven or until crisp.

To make it a complete meal, arrange some green salad, drizzle olive oil and a little apple cider vinegar on top.

Nutrition Information:
kcal: 342
Net carbs: 30g
Fat: 21g
Fiber: 7g
Protein: 5.6g

Chicken Skewers With Creamy sauce

Prep time: 10-15 minutes

Total time: 30 minutes

Servings: 1

INGREDIENTS

1 tbsp of chopped Coriander

1 tbsp of walnut butter or peanut butter

150 ml of coconut milk

50 ml of chicken stock

1 tsp of ground turmeric

1 tsp of curry powder

1 tsp of extra virgin olive oil

1 garlic clove, chopped

20 grams of red onion, diced

4 chopped walnut halves, to garnish

30 grams of sliced Celery

30 grams of kale, stalks removed and sliced

50 grams of buckwheat

1/2 tsp of extra virgin olive oil

1 tsp of ground turmeric

150 grams of chicken breast, cut into chunks

INSTRUCTIONS

1. Mix the olive oil and turmeric in a bowl, add chicken pieces and marinate for 30-90 minutes, depending on how much time you have.

2. Cook the buckwheat as instructed in packet directions, add the celery and kale about 5 minutes to the final cooking time. Drain.

3. Prepare the grill for maximum heat.

4. Heat the olive oil in a frying pan, add red onion and garlic and gently fry for 2–3 minutes until tender. Stir in the spices and keep cooking for a minute. Add coconut milk and chicken stock and bring to the boil, add in the walnut butter, stirring until well combined. Turn heat down and let it simmer for 8–10 minutes or until the sauce is creamy and rich.

5. Meanwhile, pierce skewers through chicken and grill for both sides 10 minutes.

To serve, mix the coriander into the sauce and spread sauce on top skewers, top with chopped walnuts.

Cocoa Cupcakes With Icing

Prep time: 5 minutes

Ready time: 35 minutes

Servings: 12

INGREDIENTS

120 ml of boiling water

1 egg

50 ml of vegetable oil

½ tsp of vanilla extract

120 ml of milk

½ tsp of fine espresso coffee, decaf if preferred

½ tsp of salt

60 grams of cocoa

200 grams of caster sugar

150 grams of self-raising flour

For the icing:

50 grams of soft cream cheese

½ tsp of vanilla bean paste

1 tbsp of matcha green tea powder

50 grams of icing sugar

50 grams of butter, at room temperature

INSTRUCTIONS

1. Heat your oven to 180C. Line your cupcake tin with silicone cake cases or paper.

2. In a large bowl, mix together the flour, cocoa, sugar, espresso powder and salt; mix thoroughly.

3. Beat the egg, milk, vegetable oil and vanilla extract in a bowl. In another bowl, combine the dry ingredients. Add the wet and dry ingredients together and beat with an electric mixer until fully combined.

4. Slowly pour in the hot water and whisk over low speed until nicely combined. Beat further on high speed for a minute or so to

inflate the batter. (This batter is not as thick as normal cake mix but will still turn out fine)

5. Evenly pour the cake mix between the cupcake cases, about ¾ full.

6. Place in the oven and bake for 15-18 minutes, until cake is firm and bounces back when tapped. Withdraw and set aside to completely cool before icing

7. Combine together the butter, icing sugar and cream until smooth. Add in the vanilla and matcha powder and stir again. Lastly pour the cream cheese and whisk until mixture is smooth. Pour into a piping bag and Pipe over the cakes.

Nutrition Information:
kcal: 240
Net carbs: 26g
Fat: 10.14g
Fiber: 0.7g
Protein: 3.42g

Easy Sirtfood Bites

Ready time: 65 minutes

Servings: 15-20 bites

INGREDIENTS

1 tsp vanilla extract or the scraped seeds of 1 vanilla pod

1 tbsp of extra virgin olive oil

1 tbsp of ground turmeric

1 tbsp of cocoa powder

250g of pitted Medjool dates

30g of dark chocolate or cocoa nibs (85% cocoa solids), broken into pieces

120g of walnuts

1–2 tbsp of water

INSTRUCTIONS

1. Pulse the chocolate and walnuts in a food processor until texture resembles a fine powder.

2. Add the vanilla extract, ground turmeric, cocoa powder, olive oil and Medjool dates and pulse until a ball is formed. Add water if the consistency is sticky.

3. Mold the mixture with your hands into bite-sized balls, transfer into an airtight container and refrigerate for at least 60 minutes before consuming.

If desired, coat balls in cocoa or desiccated coconut. You can store in your fridge for up to 1 week.

Nutrition Information:

kcal: 87

Net carbs: 10g

Fat: 4.77g

Fiber: 1.5g

Protein: 1.31g

Roasted Salad

Prep time: 10 minutes

Cook time: 10 minutes

Servings: 4

INGREDIENTS

1 bunch (about 20 grams) of parsley

3 medium scallions, cut into fine rings

2 medium (about 150 grams) carrots

¼ tsp of ground coriander

¼ tsp of ground cumin

½ tsp of red chili flakes, more or less to taste

Juice of 1 lemon, more to taste

1 ½ tbsp of brown sugar, more to taste

2 finely grated cloves garlic

2 tbsp of olive oil

325 ml of vegetable broth

170 grams of buckwheat groats, rinse

Fine sea salt and black pepper

INSTRUCTIONS

1. Add the vegetable broth to a saucepan and bring to a boil over medium heat. Add in the buckwheat, cover with a lid and let it simmer over low heat for about 8-10 minutes until the buckwheat is cooked as desired. Or cook according the package instructions. Its best to check 2-3 minutes before the indicated time on packed so you don't have an over cooked buckwheat. Drain and set aside to cool.

2. Mix together the garlic, olive oil, ground coriander, ¾ lemon juice, brown sugar, chili flakes, salt and pepper in a small bowl. Taste and adjust with lemon juice, sugar and salt if needed.

3. Finely chop the parsley along with the thin stem and use the bigger holes on a grater box to grate the carrots.

4. Add the carrots, scallion, parsley and buckwheat together in a bowl. Toss with the dressing and serve.

Nutrition Information:
kcal: 176
Net carbs: 9g
Fat: 7g
Fiber: 2.7g
Protein: 3g

Tuna And Avocado Kale Stuffed Snacks

Prep time: 15 minutes
Cook time: 10 minutes
Serving: 2

INGREDIENTS:
1 avocado, pitted and halved
1 teaspoon of soy sauce
1 teaspoon of extra virgin olive oil
1 tablespoon of chopped scallion, green onion
114 grams of white tuna, canned in water, drained
1 cup of finely chopped Kale

INSTRUCTIONS
1. Pour olive oil into a sauté pan and sauté the scallions for 3 to 4 minutes. Stir in tuna and sauté for 2 more minutes.
2. Add in the soy sauce and kale. Cover and cook for 3 to 4 minutes.
3. Fill each avocado half with the mixture.

Nutrition Information:
kcal: 310
Net carbs: 7g
Fat: 21g
Fiber: 8g
Protein: 19g

Cucumber Tuna Snacks

Prep time: 15 minutes

Cook time: 0 minutes

Serving: 12

INGREDIENTS:

1 can of white tuna, canned in water, drained

1 whole fresh lime juice (divided)

1 minced garlic clove

2 teaspoon of extra virgin olive oil

1 (12 sliced) cucumber

3 tomato cherry tomatoes (for garnish)

3 tomatoes diced cherry Tomatoes

1 pinch of salt and pepper

1 peeled, pitted avocado

INSTRUCTIONS

1. Mix the olive oil, drained tuna, and half lime juice together in a small bowl; season with pepper and salt. Set aside.

2. Mash the remaining lime juice and avocado flesh in a different small bowl with fork until partially smooth. Mix in diced tomatoes and minced garlic. Season mixture with salt and pepper to taste.

3. Lay out cucumber slices on a tray. Spoon small tuna mixture on each cucumber slices; add quarter cherry tomato on top, serving in tray and enjoy!

Nutrition Information:

kcal: 70

Net carbs: 2g

Fat: 4.14g

Fiber: 2.3g

Protein: 4.84g

Malabar Sirtfood Prawns

Prep time: 10 minutes

Cook time: 8 minutes

Serving: 4-6

INGREDIENTS:

½ small bunch of coriander, leaves only

40 grams of fresh coconut, grated

1 tsp of cracked black pepper

1 finely sliced onion

2-4 green chillies, halved and deseeded

4 curry leaves

1 tbsp of olive oil

40 grams of ginger divided, peeled the first and grate, finely sliced the second half into matchsticks

4 tsp of juice of lemon, plus a squeeze

3-4 tsp of Kashmiri chilli powder

2 tsp turmeric

400 grams of raw king prawns, rinse and pat dry

INSTRUCTIONS

1. Add the prawns in a bowl and toss with the chilli powder, turmeric, grated ginger, lemon juice and set aside.

2. Heat the olive oil in a frying pan and add onion, curry leaves, sliced ginger and chilli. Cook about 10 mins until fragrance and translucent, then add in black pepper.

3. Add in the prawns and stir-fry about 2 mins until cooked. Taste and adjust season if needed; add a squeeze of lemon juice. Serve sprinkled with the coriander leaves and grated coconut.

Nutrition Information:
kcal: 171
Net carbs: 4g
Fat: 8g
Fiber: 3g
Protein: 19g

Printed in Great Britain
by Amazon

48354184R00071